The
Channel Four Racing
Guide to
RACEHORSES

CHANNEL FOUR RACING GUIDES

edited by Sean Magee

already published

FORM AND BETTING

with Jim McGrath and John McCririck

RACECOURSES

with Derek Thompson

The
Channel Four Racing
Guide to
RACEHORSES

with
JOHN FRANCOME
and members of the Channel Four Racing team

edited by
SEAN MAGEE

First published in 1999 by Channel 4 Books, an imprint of Macmillan
Publishers Ltd, 25 Eccleston Place, London SW1W 9NF and Basingstoke

Associated companies throughout the world.

ISBN 0 7522 1399 7

9 8 7 6 5 4 3 2

A CIP catalogue record for this book is available from the British Library.

Commissioning Editor: Susanna Wadeson
Editor: Gillian Bromley
Design and production by Production Line
Printed by Mackays of Chatham plc, Chatham, Kent

This book accompanies the television series Channel Four Racing
made by Highflyer Productions for Channel 4.
Executive producers: John Fairley and Andrew Franklin

Contents

Acknowledgements

The photographs in the colour section between pages 96 and 97 are all by George Selwyn, with the following exceptions: the pictures of Remittance Man with Nobby and of Cadeaux Genereux are by Trevor Jones, and of Spanish Steps by Stephen Cannon.

The line drawings for 'Points of the horse' on page 28 and 'Equipment' on pages 78–9 are by Jackie Hunt.

Thanks to Steve Cannon not only for that Spanish Steps photograph but also for extensive advice about the horse and its imperfections. Thanks also to all the Channel Four Racing team (especially GG, for a crash course in pronunciation) and to Verity Willcocks, Phillip Jones, Gillian Bromley and Charlie Webster.

Preface

You can't have horse racing without horses, and the aim of this *Channel Four Racing Guide to Racehorses* is simply to dispense some basic information about the true stars of the racing game.

Everyone with the slightest interest in racing has some concern for horses themselves – on a spectrum which stretches from viewing them as mere conveyances of your stake money, little more than an animated (in some cases not nearly animated enough) casino chip, to awe at their power, athleticism and sheer beauty. Firmly at the latter end of that spectrum is the editor of this book, who likes nothing more than tracking down famous old racehorses and oozing sentimentality over the field gate.

A knowledge of what makes a racehorse is one of the fundamental requirements of any successful punter, and this *Guide* begins with a comprehensive rundown of what to look for in a horse by John Francome, while insights on horse-watching from all the Channel Four Racing presenters follow throughout.

All text not signed by John or one of the other presenters is by Sean Magee, and in some parts is adapted or amplified from previous editions of *The Channel Four Book of Racing*.

S.M.

Catching the eyecatchers
John Francome's guide to horse spotting

The close study of racehorses can be profitable as well as pleasurable, for the physical appearance of any horse before a race will tell you a great deal about its chances.

The knack, of course, is to know what to look for, but it is also vital to appreciate that different types of physical specimen are suited to different types of race: to take extreme examples, you wouldn't expect anything in the Grand National field to look like a runner in a five-furlong handicap.

Preliminaries

If you're at the races, try to get to the pre-parade ring rather than going straight to the paddock rail: there is less bustle than in the paddock itself, and you're likely to get a better chance of a long hard look at each horse. At many courses the pre-parade ring has an atmosphere all its own: the July Course at Newmarket, for example, where the runners walk round in the shade of tall trees, or the spacious pre-parade at Sandown Park.

But whether you're watching on television or in the flesh, start by considering a few basic points:

- As with any athlete, assessing the overall physical condition of a horse is partly a matter of subjective judgement. But generally you're looking for a horse with an intelligent and alert outlook and a bold eye (or, ideally, two!). Many horse-watchers take great account of the ears, as long ears supposedly indicate genuineness and courage. ('Lop' ears which flop forwards are traditionally a sign of an exceptionally genuine character.) The ears should point slightly inwards. The carriage of the head should be high, and the shoulder well sloped to give maximum drive to the forelegs. The neck should be well muscled. A deep chest is a good sign – lots of room for heart and lungs – but always avoid flab: like any human, a horse with too much of a tummy is not fit. A fit horse exudes muscularity and power, just like a fit human athlete. The back should be on the short rather than the long side and the quarters – the powerhouse of the equine system – round and full of muscle. A good tip is to check a horse from behind: look for the 'hard marks' – grooves either side of the tail – that indicate peak muscular condition.

- In the summer you'll want your fancy to have a shiny, well-groomed coat: a 'stary' coat – dull and patchy – is not a good sign. Always stand with the sun behind you. View each horse from an identical angle. It's uncanny how the horse with the healthiest looking coat invariably runs the best.

- Look for the signs which indicate whether a horse is likely to act on the prevailing going. Large feet are often suited to soft going, small feet to firmer ground.

- How does the horse walk? It is often said that a horse that walks well will gallop well, and you can learn a lot from the walking action about how an individual will use himself in the faster paces. Look for a fluid gait, where the horse is covering a good deal of ground with every stride. Try to see if he is 'tracking up', with the hind foot overlapping or falling in front of the print left by the front foot on the same side. This is easier said than done, especially if you are watching on television, but in any case concentrate on whether the horse is walking loosely and easily or clattering round with a more mincing stride. The latter does not of course mean that the horse will not win – some fine horses have not been good walkers – but as a rule a loose walk is a much better sign than a more constricted gait. Listen as they walk by: you can hear the plodders. In studying the walk, as in all other aspects of assessing horses, the more you do it the better you'll get at it.

- If the horse is jig-jogging round the paddock rather than walking calmly beside its handler, consider why. Horses that do this seldom run well in staying races, where a calm and resolute demeanour usually pays dividends. In most cases the bobbing up and down is a sign of keenness, but sometimes it's an indication of jangling nerves. How do you know which? Since the horse is not available for a pre-race interview, you have to deduce what you can of his mental state from his physical condition. Have a good, lingering look to check whether there appear to be signs of agitation. Disinclination to be led round quietly – pulling against his handler – is one telling sign, as are twitching the ears and swishing the tail.

  Another is sweating. Some horses sweat up before a race in sheer anticipation of what lies ahead, and should not be discounted on those grounds. With others, sweating is definitely a bad sign, as it indicates that the horse is wasting nervous energy and will not be able to give his best in the race. Normally, sweating around the ears and eyes is not encouraging. A lather of frothy sweat between the back legs is a certain sign the animal will not run to its best. Sweating on the neck, on the other hand, is often a sign of keenness (a bit like an actor getting keyed up before a performance). And, at the risk of stating the obvious, bear in mind that on a very hot day any horse is much more likely to be sweating than on a cold day . . .

  Most importantly, get to know your horses. With some, such as that terrific miler of a few years back Zilzal, you're worried if they're *not* sweating.

- As well as having a close look at the runners in the paddock, try to watch them going down to the start. You can see from how a horse strides out whether he is liking the ground. On firm ground, the horse who goes to post gingerly or in a scrtachy fashion is not likely to want to exert himself and stretch out on that surface in the race. A high knee action often indicates a liking for wet ground, a daisy-cutting action the opposite. But whatever the going, the real eye-catcher is the horse who seems to float over the ground, expending the minimum energy to cover the maximum distance.

Although these fundamentals are always worth bearing in mind, remember that different considerations apply at different times of year and at different stages of the season.

A horse grows a winter coat, so you can't expect a chaser in early February to be gleaming with condition. When towards the end of the Flat season in the autumn a filly or mare starts to 'go in her coat' – that is, grow her winter coat – she will often start to lose her form, though the same does not necessarily apply to the male of the species.

For runners on the Flat, the autumn is the period when there is always the risk of 'going over the top' – becoming generally fed up with the whole business of racing, and thus disinclined to run to form. Physical symptoms of a horse going over the top can include sweating up, dull coat, twitchy, irritated behaviour or a general air of lethargy and listlessness. A horse who looks tucked up under his belly – who has 'run up light' – is unlikely to be at his best. But all too often his disenchantment is not obvious until after a poor run in the race itself.

Come the spring, the situation is very different.

Most horses thrive with the sun on their backs, and in the early months of the Flat season a horse who has lost its winter coat is likely to be more forward than one who has not: this can apply especially to fillies and mares.

Beyond the generalities, it's important to have some sense of what to look for in different types of horse running in different types of race.

Two-year-olds

It's sometimes thought that two-year-olds who make their racecourse debuts early in the season – April or May – are likely to be too precocious to figure in the middle-distance Classics the following year, but that's not necessarily the case. Of Derby winners in the 1990s, both Generous and Dr Devious made their first racecourse appearances as two-year-olds in May. Commander In Chief, on the other hand, did not race at all as a juvenile. Moral: there's no hard-and-fast rule.

When assessing a two-year-old, bear in mind his breeding. If his sire was a late developer (Mtoto, for example), he might well follow suit and cannot be expected to be precocious. Also consider the date on which the horse was foaled. Say a race is being run on 28 April. One first-time-out runner was foaled on 28 February, another on 28 May. Both are formally two-year-olds, but the first horse is already well into his third year, while the other is not actually two yet.

It is very common for a two-year-old to be 'backward' first time out – and even second time out – and a horse with an early foaling date is likely to be more forward.

Paddock-side, bear in mind that a two-year-old is a very immature racehorse indeed, and different parts of the physique develop at different rates. Early in the season a juvenile may appear very leggy, but if he is none the less walking well, that's a significant plus point.

The rear end of the horse is the power pack, and the more there is behind the saddle, even in an immature juvenile, the better. Remember Richard Hannon's wonderful tribute to his terrific two-year-old filly Lyric Fantasy: 'She has a backside on her like a scullery maid's – and the head of a model.' That bottom powered Lyric Fantasy to victory as the first two-year-old filly ever to win the Nunthorpe Stakes, York's great sprint race: no wonder she was called 'The Pocket Rocket'.

Another factor to accord particular weight when looking at two-year-olds is temperament. That first racecourse appearance is a very strange experience for the raw recruit: study how he reacts to his surroundings. Does he take it all in his stride, or is he whinnying for reassurance from his fellows? Worrying wastes energy.

Try to get a good look as the jockey is legged up: a good jockey is usually a calming influence on a nervous horse. Then watch as the runners leave the paddock: does the horse try to go sideways, or walk straight on as a good horse should? Stand by where the runners come out on to the course: some will be less than keen to set off for the start, while others will get on with it like old pros.

In the race itself, watch for signs of 'greenness' – the inexperience which in a young horse can make all the difference between losing and winning. The most obvious sign of greenness is when a horse, baffled by the novelty of taking part in a race, finds it impossible to concentrate on the matter in hand and gets distracted. He may 'change his legs' – that is, alter his stride pattern – and become unbalanced. He may start to look at the crowd and wander off a true line, or simply take too long to realise that he should be putting his head down and galloping to the line. Most horses learn quickly and few display symptoms of greenness for more than a couple of outings. If a horse continues to decline to knuckle down when it matters, that is not greenness but unreliability – another matter entirely.

Three-year-olds

The most significant time to study a high-class three-year-old – one with Classic pretensions – is before his first race of the season, and the crucial question to be addressed then is: has he trained on? Some horses are at their peak as two-year-olds and never go on to fulfil all that promise they showed as juveniles. In recent memory Arazi is a case in point. His sensational victory in the 1991 Breeders' Cup Juvenile at Churchill Downs proclaimed him one of the greats, but he never hit the heights at three, winning two races but failing when it mattered most in the Kentucky Derby.

A racehorse is considered to have 'trained on' if he has developed and matured from two to three, and when looking at a Classic candidate early in the season ask yourself: has he grown significantly since last year, does he look mature and solidly built, or, compared with other horses, does he still look small?

Sprinters

What you're principally looking for in a sprinter is power – an impression of pent-up energy which, once unleashed as the stalls open, will catapult the horse off at top speed. The classic sprinting type will be very strong behind the saddle, full of sheer muscular propulsion. Along with that explosive quality, however, must go a degree of control. A sprinter who gets overwrought in paddock or parade and carts his jockey on the way to the start is likely to have shot his bolt before the race begins, and many is the time punters have backed a hot favourite only to see him throw his chance away on the way to post. If only they'd waited a few more minutes before getting on . . . Moral: whatever the form book says, studying a horse in the paddock and going down provides vital information. Ignore it at your peril!

Chasers and hurdlers

In recent years a marked difference in National Hunt horses seems to have emerged between the 'old-fashioned' type of jumping horse, like Jodami or Dublin Flyer – strong, tall, very well made – and the smaller sort of horse who has probably been bred for the Flat, and in many cases has raced on the Flat: many of Martin Pipe's hurdlers, for example, or recent Champion Hurdlers such as Alderbrook and Istabraq. These Flat-breds are a size smaller than the traditional chasing type, lighter of bone and more spare in conformation; many of them remain hurdlers throughout their racing careers, whereas the traditional type tended to start out over the smaller obstacles and then progress to fences.

The lighter sort of horse tends to take less getting fit, whereas most of the leading chasers need at least a couple of races to reach top condition and should be approached cautiously until you're sure they're on song. Big chasers always take time to get going in the first stages of the season, and cannot be rushed.

Remember, too, that horses who have graduated to hurdling from the Flat are often unsuited to the very heavy ground which can prevail in the depths of winter, and firmer going tends to be more to the liking of lightly made horses.

The great advantage which the winter game has over the Flat, at least from the point of view of careful students of horseflesh, is that you can get much more familiar with individual horses as they run season after season. Once you have come to know a horse well, you can more readily tell whether he is on top form or not. When Dublin Flyer came into the parade ring before the Tripleprint Gold Cup at Cheltenham in 1994 he looked perfection in a chaser: tall, strong, immensely well muscled, gleaming in his coat, eager and on his toes, anxious to get on with it but keeping all his energy under control. He duly won. With that picture in your mind, you could always relate his chance in a subsequent race to how far he matched that condition: when he fell a little short of it, he did not do so well.

Old Night Nurse, who died recently, used to amble round the parade ring as if a race were the last thing on his mind: but once you were aware that this was simply the horse's character, his apparent lethargy would never put you off. It was the same with Mr Frisk and his sweating. The more he sweated the better he ran, and once you knew that you could judge the condition of the horse against your mental yardstick.

But there is a problem with paddock inspection in the winter. Rugs. On a cold day a horse is going to be protected against the elements until the last possible moment, with a rug over his quarters even after the jockey has mounted, so it pays to take up a position near the paddock exit and get a look at each horse at that last moment as they go out on to the course.

Also in the winter, take account of clipping. A racehorse's coat is clipped regularly throughout the cold months to keep him as cool as possible in the places where he will sweat the most. 'Clipping out' leaves just the legs and the saddle area unclipped, while 'trace clipping' leaves the winter coat on most of the neck and back. A more limited clip can disguise a horse's condition – though it won't hide the fat tummy of a horse not yet in tip-top shape.

Behaviour in running

If you are interested in a particular horse, watch him as carefully as you can during the race itself to build a fuller picture of his nature and character, and learn lessons for the future.

The horse who pulls hard and fights his rider is wasting energy which would be better used trying to run faster than his rivals, while the horse who can be persuaded to settle is much more likely to last the trip. Horses cannot be imbued with stamina which they do not naturally possess, but they can, by patient training, be taught to harness their reserves of energy and become much more amenable in a race.

It is characteristic of many horses to stop once they reach the front. There is nothing necessarily ungenuine in this: the horse is a herd animal and many do not wish to get too far detached from their fellows. Sea Pigeon, on whom I had an armchair ride to win the Champion Hurdle in 1981, tended to idle once in the lead, and the trick was to produce him at the last possible moment. Whatever claims we may make for their intelligence, a horse does not know where the winning post is, and may well think he has done all that is required once he gets his head in front.

Try to get another look at the horse after the race. Win or lose, the contest itself will have taken something out of the participant, and a measure of just how much can be gauged from how he is breathing immediately after the race. If he is blowing hard, that suggests that he was not at prime fitness, and significant improvement can be expected in subsequent races.

Final suggestions

- Never force yourself to like a horse. There's always another race, and you'll be kicking yourself if you back a loser when you know deep down that you didn't like what you saw in the paddock.
- Pay attention to which horse wins the 'Best Turned Out' award which is now a parade ring feature of so many races. Often the best turned out proves to be the winner, and this is no coincidence.
- Familiarise yourself with individual horses as much as you can. The more you know, the more useful will be the evidence of your own eyes.
- Flat or jumps, paddock observation is most effective in the early part of the season when fitness is both at a premium and most obvious to the beholder.
- Bear in mind that different physical types are suited by different races. If before a race you like two horses equally, go for the one better built for the job in hand.

Good luck – and see you paddock-side!

John Francome

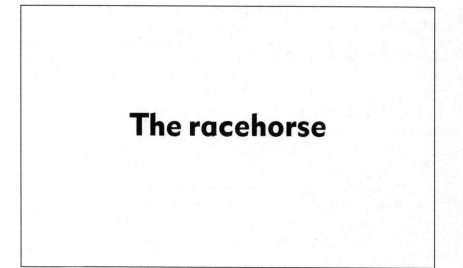

The racehorse

HORSE SENSE from Brough Scott . . .

Mill Reef was the beau ideal. When he moved, he seemed to float across the ground – and that was just at the walk.

At its heart, horse racing is no more and no less than equine athletics. What you need to see in a horse is an athlete who seems ready and capable of running a hole in the wind for you.

Picture for yourself what you would like a great athlete to look like limbering up: the head alert and focused, the body loose and lithe. Above all, get an image of a great stride like Mill Reef's or, more recently, Nashwan's, and see if your fancy can compare just a little.

What you need is a mover.

. . . and Graham Goode

From the commentary box I've seen lots of horses move to the start. An easy, flowing stride on good ground shouts that the horse is on good terms with itself. Fluent movers are easy to identify and really fill the eye.

In the race, a low head carriage seems to indicate a willing runner. A dour stayer like Further Flight is an excellent example: it was as if his nose was magnetised to the ground.

Beware horses that act out of character and be cautious about horses that jig-jog and sweat badly.

The racehorse

First get the names right:

- A horse at birth is a foal, a colt if male and a filly if female. Its father is its sire and its mother its dam. A horse is 'by' its sire and 'out of' its dam – thus Swain is by Nashwan out of Love Smitten by Key To The Mint (Key To The Mint being the sire of Love Smitten).
- The official birthday of every racehorse in the northern hemisphere is 1 January, and at the start of the year after its birth the foal becomes a yearling – even though it will be short of its biological birthday by anything from a single day to several months. A year later it becomes a two-year-old, a year after that a three-year-old, and so on. At the age of five a colt becomes a horse, and a filly a mare.
- Another horse sharing the same dam is its half-brother (or half-sister): for example, Marju, second to Generous in the 1991 Derby, was a half-brother of 1990 One Thousand Guineas winner Salsabil – they were both out of the dam Flame Of Tara.
- Another horse sharing the same sire and dam is its full brother (or full sister): Morley Street and Granville Again, Champion Hurdle winners in 1991 and 1993 respectively, were full brothers, by Deep Run out of High Board.
- However, another horse sharing the same sire but not the same dam is not described as its half-brother (or half-sister).

- Two colts who share a dam and a paternal grandsire are known as three-parts brothers. For example: Commander Collins, winner of the Racing Post Trophy in 1998, is a three-parts brother to Colonel Collins, third in both Two Thousand Guineas and Derby in 1994. They share the dam Kanmary and each is by a son of Northern Dancer – El Gran Senor in the case of Colonel Collins, Sadler's Wells in the case of Commander Collins.

Private parts

A gelding is a horse that has been castrated (in racing jargon, 'cut'). The operation commonly takes place in the autumn of the horse's second year, although many others are gelded after their racing performances have shown that they have little future at stud. The gelding operation is performed under sedation and then local anaesthetic, using a clamping and cutting device, and is quite painless.

Arcadian Heights became the first gelding to win a Group One race in Great Britain when taking the Ascot Gold Cup in 1994.

An ungelded horse is sometimes called an entire, or a 'full' horse. Chasing entires, especially notably successful ones, are few and far between: Fortina won the Cheltenham Gold Cup in 1947, and the last entire to win the Grand National was Battleship in 1938. (The good two-mile chaser Kadastrof is an entire.) Over hurdles, where the horses tend to be younger and the obstacles are easier to negotiate, entires are somewhat more common, among them some top performers: Monksfield, for instance, won two Champion Hurdles before embarking on a stud career abbreviated by his death in 1989, and the 1995 Champion Hurdle was won by Alderbrook, who is now standing at stud. Of course, geldings do not run only under National Hunt Rules, and though they may not take part in the Classics (the rationale being that for the good of the breed all Classic winners should be able to pass on their qualities), most of the big Flat races are now open to them, and old geldings such as Teleprompter or Further Flight won a place in the affections of the racing public unmatched by all but a very few Classic winners, however brilliant their transient glory.

It may seem strange that the likes of Desert Orchid or One Man could not procreate, but had they not been gelded they would not have achieved what they did in steeplechasing. While the common explanation for gelding a potential chaser – that the 'full' horse might be understandably reluctant to launch himself over four and a half feet of packed birch – is certainly plausible, of more pressing relevance is that an entire is likely to have his mind on other things as he matures and will find it difficult to stand up to the wintry rigours of the jumping game – or, indeed, a prolonged racing life on the Flat.

Aurelius, winner of the 1961 St Leger, was returned to racing after proving unsuccessful at stud. Gelded and sent jumping, he won over hurdles and fences and ran second in the 1967 Champion Hurdle, only to be disqualified for hanging on the run-in.

Sometimes it happens that only one testicle descends in a colt. These horses are called 'rigs' and, not surprisingly, are often rather difficult characters. Selkirk, a very good miler of the early 1990s, was a rig, and his form improved markedly once the troublesome gland had been removed. After his victory over Kooyonga in the Queen Elizabeth II Stakes at Ascot in 1991, the filly's trainer Michael Kauntze offered an apt comment about the winner, reported in the following Monday's *Racing Post*: 'If I'd been running around all my life with an inflamed testicle and it was suddenly sorted out, I'm sure I'd run faster.'

An entire at stud is a stallion, and a mare used for breeding is a broodmare.

Early days

A Thoroughbred foal is born after a gestation period of around eleven months, will stand for the first time within an hour of being born, and will suck from its dam within two hours. Very soon after

birth it will have its first experience of running – a natural development in a creature whose basic motivation is flight from predators:
there's no time to lie around enjoying being a baby.

The foal has a close bond with its dam in the early months but
shows increasing independence before being weaned at about five
months old.

Thoroughbreds born twins are rare, for while as many as 30 per cent
of conceptions result in twins, in most cases the vet will 'pop' one of
the eggs to ensure that only one foal is born. The reasoning behind
this is that each twin would probably be significantly weaker than a
single offspring, though there have been examples of successful
racing twins.

Age

The Thoroughbred racehorse matures at about five, but on the Flat it
has tended to be unusual for a top-class horse to continue racing
beyond the age of four, since the fees which a top-class horse can
command as a stallion exceed the likely prize money to be earned by
continuing racing.

That said, there has been an encouraging trend in recent years for a
few of the best horses to be kept in training at five or even six, sometimes
with spectacular results:

- Six-year-old Swain became the oldest horse ever to win the
  King George VI and Queen Elizabeth Diamond Stakes at
  Ascot when beating High-Rise in the 1998 race. This victory
  also made him only the second horse ever to win the King
  George twice (the first being Dahlia in 1973 and 1974),
  following his defeat of Pilsudski and Helissio in 1997.
- Singspiel won the Dubai World Cup, Coronation Cup and
  International Stakes in 1997 at the age of five.
- Pilsudski, having won the Breeders' Cup Turf at four,
  excelled himself at five, winning the Eclipse Stakes, Irish

Champion Stakes, Champion Stakes and Japan Cup in 1997.

- Cigar (see page 113) was six when he won the inaugural Dubai World Cup in 1996.

Such cases are still the exception, as most owners of the very best horses understandably want to maximise the earning potential of their charges by getting them off to stud when they are at the top of the market and can command high covering fees. Equally understandably, racegoers want to watch the top horses in action for as long as they can, and the chance of seeing the likes of Pilsudski, Swain and Singspiel on the track well beyond what might have been seen as their sell-by dates has made the Flat scene infinitely more interesting to racing fans than it was when star performers were prematurely retired.

Quest For Fame is the only Derby winner this century to have won a race at the age of five: he moved to the United States as a four-year-old in 1991 and won the Hollywood Turf Handicap at Hollywood Park, California, in 1992.

The youngest age at which horses race on the Flat is two; they can race over hurdles at three and over fences at four. A two-year-old on the Flat, or a hurdler running at three in the autumn or four in the spring, is often referred to as a 'juvenile'. All the English Classics (Two Thousand Guineas, One Thousand Guineas, Oaks, Derby and St Leger) are confined to three-year-olds.

When winning the Prix de l'Abbaye at Longchamp in October 1998, eight-year-old My Best Valentine became the oldest horse to win a Group One race on the Flat in Europe since the Pattern was introduced in 1971.

The status of 'novice' has nothing directly to do with age. In jump racing, a 'novice' is a horse who has not won a race under that particular

Life cycle of a racehorse – Entrepreneur

- Spring 1993: Entrepreneur's dam Exclusive Order is covered by the stallion Sadler's Wells at the Coolmore Stud in Ireland.
- 7 March 1994: Exclusive Order gives birth to a bay colt foal.
- 1 January 1995: although not yet ten months old, Entrepreneur formally becomes a yearling.
- September 1995: the colt is sold at the Houghton Sales, Newmarket, for 600,000 guineas (joint top price of the sale) to owner Michael Tabor and is sent into training with Michael Stoute at Newmarket.
- 2 August 1996: Entrepreneur's first race as a two-year-old, a maiden stakes at Newmarket: he starts odds-on favourite but finishes fourth.
- 21 August 1996: in his second race, a maiden at Kempton Park, he again starts odds-on, this time justifying the price by winning easily.
- 25 September 1996: in his third race, at Chester, he starts at 6–1 on and wins impressively.
- 3 May 1997: the Two Thousand Guineas at Newmarket, his first race as a three-year-old: he starts second favourite and wins by three-quarters of a length from the favourite Revoque.
- 7 June 1997: starts odds-on favourite for the Derby but can finish only fourth behind Benny The Dip.
- 27 September 1997: starts second favourite for the Queen Elizabeth II Stakes at Ascot but is unplaced.
- 10 October 1997: it is announced that Entrepreneur has been retired after just six races and will not run again.
- Spring 1998: Entrepreneur takes up stallion duties at Coolmore, where he was bred. His offspring will first be seen on a racecourse in 2001.

code – hurdling or steeplechasing – before 1 May of the previous season; so a horse who won a chase in late May 1998 would still be able to run as a novice during the 1998–9 season. Those for whom wins prove elusive retain the tag long after their youth is past: Panegyrist lost his novice status in a chase at Ayr in March 1989 at the ripe old age of fourteen.

On the Flat, any horse running at six years old or over is thought to be fairly long in the tooth, though steeplechasers will carry on typically to about twelve – often beyond – and are usually held to be in their prime at eight or nine. Oldest horse this century to win the Grand National was Sergeant Murphy, thirteen when landing the 1923 running.

There is no record of a horse in Britain winning a race at older than eighteen, and of those who have scored at that venerable age special mention must be made of Wild Aster, who in 1919, in his nineteenth year, won three hurdle races in the space of a week. More familiar to current racing fans is the memory of Sonny Somers, a grand old chaser trained by Fred Winter who won twice in 1980 at eighteen.

The oldest horse to have taken part in a race in Britain is Creggmore Boy, who ran in the Furness Selling Handicap Chase at Cartmel in June 1962 at the age of twenty-two: he finished fourth.

Thoroughbreds can live to about thirty; a few last even longer. The Australian gelding Tango Duke is reported to have been forty-two on his death in 1978. Spanish Steps, winner of the 1969 Hennessy Gold Cup and a highly popular chaser in the 1970s, had reached the exceptional age of thirty-four when he died in May 1997 (see plate opposite page 97).

Height and weight

A horse is measured at the shoulder in 'hands', a hand being four inches. The usual height for a mature Thoroughbred is around sixteen hands (five feet four inches), though some notable horses have been at the extremes of the height scale, including 1992 Grand National winner Party Politics, a giant at over eighteen hands.

A foal weighs 80–120 pounds at birth, and a mature racehorse in training hits the scales at around 1,100 pounds – three-quarters of a ton.

Weight can be a very telling indication of the race fitness and general well-being of a racehorse, and many trainers regularly check their charges on an equine weighbridge to monitor their condition and assess when a particular individual is coming to his ideal 'racing weight'. (In Japan racehorses are publicly weighed at the track and the weights announced – thus making knowledge of an individual horse's weight another weapon in the punter's betting armoury.)

On a race day, the stress of travel and the race itself can cause a horse to lose as much as forty pounds: the less weight lost, the better the horse has come out of the race.

Points of the horse

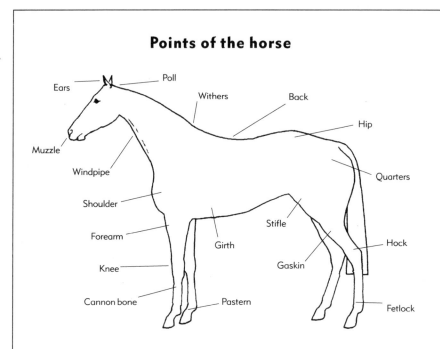

Nigel Molesworth, famed chronicler of life from the perspective of a prep school boy, considers the conformation of racehorses in *Whizz for Atomms*:

> *Every horse is said to hav POINTS which is pritty difficult for any animal which is not a hedgehog or comon porcupine. In racing, however, there are only two POINTS about the horse which need concern the eager student – the ears and the tail. If the horse is going to try the ears should be so far back and the tail so far up that they almost meet. When it trot up to the post like that the backer can be sure it is trying, which is something with a horse.*

The principal parts of the racehorse's anatomy to which you may hear reference on Channel Four Racing are indicated on the diagram above, and it is worth reminding punters that with regard to both ears and tails, Nigel Molesworth is somewhat wide of the mark.

Ears Contrary to what Molesworth says, ears laid flat back are a distinctly adverse sign – as anyone who has been approached by a malevolent horse will testify. But the ears are a very good indicator of a horse's mood. When a horse runs with his ears pricked during the closing stages of a race, he is not under excessive pressure and has something left in the tank. More worryingly, he may also have taken his mind off the job, perhaps just idling in front, perhaps distracted by the noise of the crowd. Long equine ears are considered a more positive feature than short ones, and loppy ears a sign of gameness (see John Francome on page 10 and John McCririck on page 150).

Windpipe   If a horse has been 'tubed' to remedy a breathing difficulty (see pages 95–6) you may be able to see the hole on the underside of the neck.

Shoulder   A sloping shoulder – that is, one where an imaginary line between the horse's wither and the front end of the shoulderblade ('point of the shoulder') is at a fairly wide angle from the vertical – is a definite advantage: usually a sign of a good, flowing action, it will also mean better shock absorption.

Forearm and gaskin   There are no muscles in a horse's leg below the knee; so all the power in the front leg has to come from the forearm. Sprinters in particular should be well muscled here, and also in the gaskin on the hind leg.

Back   A long back can be a sign of weakness, and it often pays to look for the more compact, 'close-coupled' animal, especially when examining sprinters. However, a larger-framed, more loosely built horse – often described as 'rangy' or 'scopey' – can be particularly effective over long distances. A youngster who appears awkwardly built or gangly – 'unfurnished' – on an early outing may well fill out and acquire better proportions.

Girth   The depth of girth in a horse is dictated by the size of his ribcage. Within reason, the deeper the better, as a capacious ribcage provides plenty of room for heart and lungs. The incomparable Arkle was a famously deep-girthed horse. But beware of the horse whose substantial size in this area is due not to his ribcage but to a lingering tummy: while some horses habitually carry a lot of 'condition' – racing euphemism for flesh – a well-padded girth generally denotes a lack of fitness. At the other extreme, beware the horse that has 'run up light' – lost too much condition – often towards the end of the season. A horse that looks less than happy as well as on the thin side is often described as 'tucked up'.

Quarters   These provide the power for each stride: the more here the better, provided it's muscle and not flab. Look for the 'hard marks' running parallel to the tail when seen from behind.

Tail   When a horse swishes his tail during a race, often though not always in irritation at being hit with the whip, many observers take it as a bad sign, thinking that he should be concentrating his energy on running as fast as he can. Yet many good horses have merrily swished their tails without any obvious lessening of their resolve: a familiar recent example is King Of Sparta, who won six chases in the first half of the 1998–9 season.

Sleep

A horse does not need to lie down to sleep, nor, being a target of predators, will it be in his interests for him to lapse into sleep for any length of time. Horses can 'lock' themselves into a position where they can sleep while standing up or leaning against a solid object such as a wall or a manger.

Colour

A Thoroughbred horse's colour is registered at birth, though colouring can occasionally change with age. The basic colours are:

- *Bay* All shades of brown, with the 'points' (muzzle, mane, tail and extremities of the legs) black. Bay is by far the most common colour found in Thoroughbreds.
- *Brown* Distinctly brown all over.
- *Black* Distinctly black all over.
- *Chestnut* A range of shades from a light golden colour to a dark 'liver' chestnut.
- *Grey* A range from pure white to dark grey. Grey horses tend to get whiter as they get older. About 3 per cent of racehorses are greys.
- *Roan* A combination of red, white and yellow or black, white and yellow hairs which gives a washy appearance. Roans are unusual in racehorses, but not unknown: the 1964 Sussex Stakes winner was one – Roan Rocket.

Colour is sometimes held to be an indication of a horse's temperament. A bright or 'flashy' chestnut (in particular a filly) is often thought to be unreliable, and there is a theory – belied by such performers as Eclipse (see page 122) and The Minstrel, an exceptionally brave winner of the Derby in 1977 under the full Lester Piggott treatment – that you cannot trust a chestnut with four white legs.

In addition to coat colour, horses are distinguishable by the white markings on their faces – usually a star, stripe or blaze. (A thin white stripe between the nostrils is called a snip.) Of these, the most striking feature is the broad expanse of a white blaze, as with Shergar, Mr Mulligan or – most spectacularly in recent favourites – Double Trigger.

Speed

Speed is the essence of racing. In the fastest modern British race on record, the Tadworth Handicap over five furlongs at Epsom on 2 June 1960, the winning horse Indigenous averaged over 41 miles per hour – though that race was timed by hand, generally regarded as less reliable than the electrical timing now in widespread use.

The average speed of 1998 Smurfit Champion Hurdle winner Istabraq was about 32 miles per hour; of Martell Grand National winner Earth Summit about 25 miles per hour (and it must be remembered that the race was run in very heavy going); of Vodafone Derby winner High-Rise about 35 miles per hour.

Horses often (though not always) speed up towards the end of a race, and the runners at the climax of a five-furlong sprint downhill on firm ground are probably clocking around 44 miles per hour.

Action

A racehorse has four basic gaits: walk, trot, canter and gallop. It is, of course, the last of these that matters most during a race, and when galloping a horse is said to 'lead' with one or other of his forelegs – that is, the leading leg is the last to touch the ground during the cycle of each individual stride. On a left-hand track a horse should lead with his near foreleg (left front leg) and on a right-hand track with his off foreleg (right front leg). A horse is said to 'change his legs' when adjusting his action during full gallop so that he is leading with the other leg, perhaps because he is uncomfortable on the ground or becoming unbalanced under pressure towards the end of a race.

As John Francome has pointed out earlier (see page 12), you can deduce from a horse's action what his preferred going might be. A horse with a 'round' action lifts his knees high during each stride and is often suited by soft ground, whereas a more daisy-cutting style, where the toes just skim the turf, points towards a preference for the firmer side.

Action also has a part to play in whether a horse is happier going left-handed or right-handed. Many are stiffer on one side and so feel more comfortable, and therefore perform better, going one way or the other.

Vision

The horse has the largest eyes of any land mammal, and uses them in a very different way from a human. Eyes set on the side rather than the front of the head afford a field of vision of very nearly 360 degrees in which to be constantly on the look-out for predators. Research has shown that each eye has an individual field of vision of 146 degrees, with a 65-degree binocular field straight ahead and a 3-degree blind spot immediately to the rear. The horse's nose creates a small blind spot on the ground in front of him – with the consequence that a horse taking a fence at speed cannot actually see the jump at the moment of take-off: he is depending on the image of that jump seen two or three strides before, on the approach. (Often a horse will turn his head slightly as he jumps.)

Blinkers or a visor (see page 79) severely reduce the field of lateral vision and thus shut out distractions, focusing the horse's sight.

Intelligence and temperament

'The good news', according to Stephen Budiansky's excellent book *The Nature of Horses*, 'is that horses have a relatively large brain for an animal of their size. The bad news is that they use most of it just to keep their feet in the right place.'

The horse's brain is about the size of an adult human fist and on average weighs around 650 grams. To put this in some sort of perspective, consider the following relative weights of brain:

    human 1,400 grams
    horse 650 grams
    cow 500 grams
    pig 125 grams

Looked at from another point of view, the brain of the average Thoroughbred horse accounts for around 0.14 per cent of body weight, compared with about 2 per cent in a human.

Whatever the brain size, what matters is what is performed and achieved with it, and the question of 'intelligence' in a horse is difficult to define.

A horse does not have the intellectual capacity to solve the Picture Puzzle or get interfered with in running as he knows he's expected at Chepstow next week; nor does he know where the winning post is. In a range of tests, horses were shown to learn approximately as quickly as tropical aquarium fish, guinea pigs and octopuses. But it has also been shown by animal behaviourists that once a horse has managed to learn something it has an excellent memory with which to retain that lesson.

To use the brain to learn is one thing. To use the brain to solve problems is a more sophisticated level of intelligence, and as problem solvers horses do not score very highly. No racegoer who has witnessed a loose horse careering around looking for the way back to the stables will be surprised to learn that when it comes to working out how to get round obstacles, horses are not in the same league as dogs, monkeys or raccoons: a well-trained collie, for example, can show great 'intelligence' in anticipating what a sheep might do. 'Much of this', writes Stephen Budiansky, 'probably has to do with the differences between carnivores and herbivores; problem solving is part of the survival kit of an animal that lives by anticipating the complex and highly varied actions of elusive prey. Mice move and hide, grass doesn't.'

But how intelligent do we want our equine heroes to be? To describe a horse as a 'thinker' is not generally intended as a compliment: rather, it implies a level of individuality which renders him suspect as a racehorse since he will be 'intelligent' enough to slow down when it hurts. In any event, once we start to talk in terms of horses thinking, or of showing courage or determination or other more specific human traits such as playing up to the crowd, we are entering dangerous territory. We cannot know what a horse is feeling or what is motivating him, and yet we have to talk of horses in human terms because there is no other suitable vocabulary. Timeform may describe Pilsudski as 'game and genuine', and Amrullah (see page 154) as 'thoroughly irresolute'; in both cases the judgement boils down to a matter of consistency, or lack of it. 'Unreliability' in a horse means that his form cannot be taken at face value every time he runs:

at some times he will run better than at others. But the whole basis of form study is shaky if horses are not consistent, and therefore consistency – or genuineness – is a quality rightly prized in a racehorse.

The key to the psychology of the racehorse is of course that it is a beast of flight: its natural instinct is to put as much distance as it can, as fast as it can, between itself and any predator. When your hero lugs himself up the Cheltenham hill, he is not trying to get to the winning post, he is trying to get away from his pursuers.

Closely allied to the issues of equine intelligence and psychology is that of temperament.

One of the most notorious equine 'thinkers' of recent years was the hurdler Derring Rose. John Francome rode him in many races, and gave this account of him in *The Race of My Life*:

That horse was a law unto himself, a real old character who used to walk backwards to the gallops with his ears pricked. My brother-in-law took him hunting once, and Derring Rose ran backwards and fell into a canal: they had to swim him down about half a mile before they could get him out where the sides weren't sheer.

In the Colt Car Corinium Hurdle at Cheltenham on New Year's Eve 1981 he dug in his heels on the way to the start, so I had to get off and lug him down to the starting area. He then tried as usual to pull himself up as we were going down the hill on the stretch away from the stands. I managed to keep him going and he caught hold of the bridle again, making up an amazing amount of ground to catch the leader Heighlin. Halfway up the run-in the mulish side of Derring Rose threatened to get the better of him, but without resorting to the whip – which would have been fatal – I managed to coax him home, and he won by three lengths. It looked like a ride of great determination and all that, but the real reason I didn't want him to stop where he first decided he might, on that downhill stretch, was that it would have taken me a bloody long time to get back to the weighing room from there.

I loved Derring Rose: he was the closest you'd ever get to having a horse talk to you, and more than any horse I ever rode, he knew what was what.

Over the centuries the racehorse has been bred principally for speed, and this refinement of a specific quality has been brought about at some cost to the overall placidity of the breed. Like physical facets, temperament is hereditary, passed on through the genes, with the result that certain sires are noted for producing horses with questionable temperament: the great Italian horse Ribot, for instance (see page 137), imprinted too many of his stock with dubious temperamental characteristics.

Thoroughbreds tend to be much more highly strung, nervous and sometimes downright perverse than breeds designed for less hectic forms of work, and their temperamental quirks can be the bane of the punter's life. A horse can effectively throw away his chance in a race by 'boiling over' – getting himself worked up into a lather of nervous agitation – during the preliminaries, and this is nowhere more nervously anticipated by connections and backers than before the Derby, where comparatively raw three-year-olds have to parade in front of a vast crowd, an experience likely to find out any chinks in their temperamental armour. Yet cast your mind back to Snow Knight: he became so worked up during the Derby parade in 1974 that he lashed out with his hind legs – demolishing a piece of running rail and depositing jockey Brian Taylor on the ground – before proceeding to land the world's premier Classic at 50–1. Temperamental behaviour does not necessarily diminish the horse's chance.

The history of racing is peppered with instances of good horses whose athletic ability is at odds with their temperament, and occasionally a volatile nature gets the upper hand.

Remember that great sprinter Lochsong. Her explosive manner of running – riding her was 'like a surfer hitting a good wave', said Frankie Dettori – endeared her to the racing public, but part of that explosiveness was a temperament geared to going as fast as she could. The same temperament got the better of her at York in August 1994 before the Nunthorpe Stakes, when she became very worked up in the parade ring, was almost uncontrollable on the way to the start, and then, having sacrificed all her energy to her nerves, ran a terrible race.

Some horses 'plant' – that is, refuse to move when called upon to do so – which can be disastrous at the start of a race. The extremely high-mettled Lammtarra had a habit of doing this out on the gallops. And do

This is what John Hislop, owner-breeder of the very great Brigadier Gerard (see page 109), had to say about temperament in his book *Breeding for Racing*:

There are several guises in which temperament is to be found. It may be straightforward bad temper, evident in biting, kicking or generally savaging, or it may be lack of courage, refusing to fight out a finish or even to race at all. Further forms are nervousness, taking the shape of stage-fright, and over-excitability, resulting in the horse 'boiling over'. Added to these are extreme laziness and uncontrollable hard pulling . . .

Probably the temperament least detrimental to racing performance is straightforward bad temper. This often goes with racing ability, while aggressiveness goes hand in hand with the will to win and, however uncomfortable for those whose task it is to groom, train or ride the horse in question, these trials may be repaid by races won . . .

The worst trait of temperament is lack of courage, since courage is one of the essential qualities of a top-class racehorse. To compensate for lack of courage, a horse must be of outstanding racing ability, so that he can win without being challenged or having to struggle. Conversely, a really brave horse will sometimes beat opponents of superior ability through sheer determination . . .

Only the racecourse test will reveal the true nature of a horse's temperament . . .

Horses who pull unduly hard fall into two categories: those who are over-excitable and those who are determined to grind the opposition into dust from the moment they leave the start. The former are of little use for racing, since they are usually spent forces long before the winning-post is reached. The latter can be formidable racehorses . . .

you remember that exasperating chaser Vodkatini, a brilliant chaser when he put his mind to it, but as often as not a surly character who would just dig in his heels and refuse to set off?

Some horses try to pull themselves up in a race when they feel that enough is enough. Remember Derring Rose (John Francome does; see above, page 34) or Riverside Boy?

Some try to bite their opponents during a race: remember Arcadian Heights and Combs Ditch on their worst behaviour?

Other notoriously mean and moody horses include the great chaser Flyingbolt – 'He would eat you as soon as look at you' was the consensus regarding his sour temperament from those in Tom Dreaper's yard with the bruises to support their view. And Celtic Shot, winner of the Champion Hurdle in 1988, had little time for this nonsense – purveyed below on page 84 – about other animals providing a calming influence. Turned out in a field, he amused himself by picking any available sheep up in his teeth and savaging it.

Those sheep would not need persuading that the Thoroughbred temperament can exact a heavy cost. Yet that very spirit is an essential part of the make-up of the racehorse – the 'high-mettled racer'. And plenty of great racehorses have had a temperament, both at home and on the track, to match their status. The peerless Arkle was serene, gentle, and kind to children – and think of what the racecourse performances of Desert Orchid or Further Flight or Double Trigger said about *their* temperament . . .

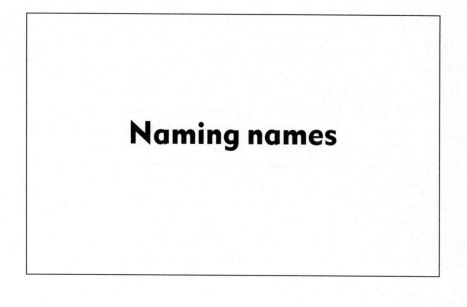

Naming names

HORSE SENSE from Derek Thompson

Horses are a bit like paintings in the sense that 'beauty is in the eye of the beholder'. Some people like greys, others like bays: it's all down to personal preference, but whatever colour and size you prefer it's the shape and make of the horse that should stand out.

I have seen some beautifully bred horses that wouldn't make the first ten in a showing class, never mind a race, so although the breeding can be a useful guide I prefer to see with my own eyes before making a decision whether to buy or bet.

My perfect horse would have plenty of shoulder muscles above his front legs and preferably a big backside that should help propel him faster than his rivals. His face should be kind, with keen, clear eyes and preferably large ears which are normally a sign of genuineness. He should look well, with a shine on his coat, and happy and at ease with the world. One look at his tummy will tell you how fit he is; indeed, if he bulges around the girth the chances are that he might well need the race. Of course, all horses are different and some run better when they are carrying condition, while others seem to enjoy jig-jogging around the parade ring and sweating up badly. I personally go against these horses, for I believe fitness is ultra-important and so is a relaxed mood that will help them put their best hoof forward.

Watch the way they canter down to the start: a horse who pounds the ground with his front legs might prefer softer going compared to a horse who shows a flowing movement. I don't like to see a horse pull his jockey down to the start, for if he is too keen he might run too freely in the race and burn himself out before the finish.

So it's all down to what you like; but if you compare horses to humans, the best advice is this. If it looks like Linford Christie, back it; if it looks like John McCririck, don't!

Naming names

Here's the result of the 3.30 at Chepchestershire, as read out by Alan Partridge – in those days a mere sports reporter – on the Radio Four programme *On the Hour*:

1 Clerical Explosion
2 Erupted Pension
3 Alanbeithtonsilboy

Few aspects of the racing scene provide quite so much harmless fun as the naming of horses. If Alanbeithtonsilboy sounds ridiculous, it is hardly more so than some of the names with which real horses have been lumbered. Fortunately, horses cannot be relied on to respond to their own names: imagine going to the field gate and calling out to Hellcatmudwrestler to come over for his lump of sugar . . .

Putting it together

Horses' names are constructed in all sorts of ways, one of the most common of which is to try to combine elements from the names of the horse's sire and dam. These elements may be words in the respective names (Florida Pearl, by Florida Sun out of Ice Pearl) or segments of the individual words (Red Rum, by Quo*rum* out of Ma*red*), or reflect aspects of their meaning, wittily construed (Lowawatha, by Dancing Brave out of Shorthouse). Then there are names which advertise a company (Gearys For Strip, Amtrak Express, Mister Baileys); names which reflect personal associations (Dorans Pride, out of Marians Pride, and owned by Tom Doran); and names which have a significance for the people who choose them that is far from obvious to anyone else.

Rules and regulations

The naming of racehorses in Great Britain is very carefully controlled by Weatherbys, the Northamptonshire-based organisation which acts as racing's civil service. Weatherbys receives applications for around 10,000 new names every year, and several criteria are strictly applied in ruling what is and is not acceptable. These include:

- *Names must not be longer than eighteen characters and spaces.* This explains those conflations, sometimes impenetrable at first sight, such as Thethingaboutitis, Blessingindisguise, Youbetterbelieveit or Dontdressfordinner – or, indeed, Alanbeithtonsilboy. A valiant attempt to grace a racehorse with that potent word from *Mary Poppins* resulted in a two-year-old in training with Barry Hills in 1997 named Supacalifragilistk.

- *Names of public personalities can be used only with written permission of that person or the family.* Sometimes it is not practical to obtain such permission. In 1984 Phil Bull, founder of Timeform, wanted to name a horse Ho Chi Minh after the North Vietnamese leader who had died in 1969. Weatherbys declined to register the name on the basis that 'Ho Chi Minh's influence and following is still strong enough to warrant such caution' – whereupon Bull, pausing only to fire a broadside at Weatherbys for refusing Ho Chi Minh but allowing Henry Kissinger, registered the horse as Ho Mi Chinh. Angelo Salvini, another of Bull's horses, was named after the head waiter at the George Hotel in Huddersfield.

Among the horses who ran on the Flat in 1998 was one Frank Le Boeuf.

- *Names cannot be made up of figures or initials.* Thus a name such as ESB, winner of the 1956 Grand National, would no longer be acceptable; however, initials can be spelled out phonetically to produce such names as Jay Em Ess or Teejay'n'aitch.

- *Names cannot start with a character other than a letter.* A horse named 'Iggins, trained by Josh Gifford, made his racecourse debut in 1995, but such a name causes problems for the computer databases on which the racing pages of newspapers so heavily rely, and 'Iggins has gone down in British racing history as a very obscure footnote: the first and only horse whose registered name begins with a mark of punctuation.

- *Names cannot be used which are already on the Register of Horse Names.* This list contains some quarter of a million currently registered names. The names thus precluded include those of any racehorse up to five years after its death or at the age of twenty, whichever is sooner; of any broodmare for ten years after her death or ten years after the last recorded year in which she foaled or was covered, or at the age of thirty, whichever is the sooner; and of any stallion fifteen years after his death or fifteen years after the last recorded year in which he covered mares, or at thirty-five years of age, whichever is the sooner.

- *Names cannot be used which are on the International and Domestic Lists of Protected Names.* These compendia protect particularly celebrated horses against their names being sullied by lesser animals in future generations. The Domestic List of Protected Names consists of the winners of

    all five English Classics
    the Ascot Gold Cup

the Grand National
the Cheltenham Gold Cup
the Champion Hurdle
the King George VI Chase

Thus you could not call your new horse Arkle – nor could you get round the rule by calling him The Arkle or Aarkle or Aachel or Ark'll, since names deemed unacceptably close to protected names are politely declined.

The list is subject to amendment – the Champion Hurdle, for instance, was added too late to prevent another Lanzarote racing in England – and cannot protect every well-known racehorse who has not won one of the specified races. Baronet was a grand old handicapper on the Flat who won the Cambridgeshire in 1978 and 1980; another Baronet is a tough grey chaser who won the 1998 Scottish National. Recent years have seen several horses whose names revived memories of not so long ago and enraged purists, including Dunkirk, Predominate, Hornbeam, Brown Lad and – horror of horrors! – Crisp. But help is at hand: a new rule prohibits the registering of 'names, in the opinion of the Stewards of the Jockey Club, of well-known horses'.

So you could not name your new acquisition Arkle or Nijinsky or Nashwan. Nor could you name him Muff Diver; though there was a sprinter bearing that curious name who raced in Ireland, Belgium (where he won several races) and Britain in the late 1970s and early 1980s, albeit never with enough distinction to get on to the International Register of Protected Names. The reason why those eagle eyebrows at Weatherbys would be raised by Muff Diver is that . . .

• *Names are not allowed 'whose meaning, pronunciation or spelling' – to quote the official Jockey Club Rule – 'may be thought obscene or insulting or, in the opinion of the Stewards of the Jockey Club, may cause offence'.* This rule has caused all sorts of complications, and all sorts of ingenuity on the part of naughty owners and trainers determined to pull a fast one over Weatherbys. Snurge, the 1990 St Leger winner whose globe-trotting exploits for a while made him the highest-earning horse in British racing history, owes his appellation to the schooldays nickname of his owner Martyn Arbib – but the horse might have had to bear a more anodyne name had a dictionary of slang been consulted before Snurge was allowed through.

Other names have successfully run the gauntlet. A two-year-old bearing the name Who Gives A Donald, trained by Colin Tinkler, ran in 1989, while Mary Hinge was an inmate of Julie Cecil's stable in the mid-1990s. (Sometimes a name has to be assessed for its potential as a Spoonerism – a phrase where the first elements of the words are swapped.)

And then there is the curious case of Wear The Fox Hat. A two-year-old filly was registered with that name and entered in a race at Folkestone in March 1995. But the Jockey Club was not comfortable with the name and insisted that an alternative be produced. She was renamed Nameless.

- *Names are not allowed which would cause confusion in the administration of racing or betting.* So don't try to name your horse 'Photo Finish', 'Stewards' Enquiry' or 'Bar'.

Horses as hoardings

The increasing use of racehorses to promote commercial organisations has led to some strange names – and plenty of publicity for the companies. The connection between horse and company may be more or less understated:

- Moorestyle, that great sprinter ridden by Lester Piggott to numerous victories in the early 1980s, was owned by Moores International Furnishings Ltd.

- Sunday Sport Star was owned by David Sullivan and used (with other similarly named horses) to promote his newspapers, while Davidgalaxy Affair and Hellcatmud-wrestler reflect Mr Sullivan's cinematic ventures.
- Mister Baileys, 1994 Two Thousand Guineas winner, was named to promote his owners Baileys Horse Feeds.
- The 'Gearys' horses – Gearys For Strip, Gearys Cold Rolled, and so on – were named for a steel finishing company.
- Plastic Spaceage, a chaser in Jim Old's yard a few years back, was owned by Spaceage Plastics Ltd, Konvekta Ltd had Konvekta King and Konvekta Queen with Oliver Sherwood, and in the late 1980s Mark Johnston trained such horses as Hinari Hi Fi, Hinari Video, Hinari Sound and Hinari Televideo for . . . wait for it! . . . Hinari Consumer Electronics Ltd. And then there's Hever Golf, Equiname, Foodbroker, Hoh, Pertemps, Eurolink, Jet . . .

Causes of confusion

A complicating factor in the naming of racehorses, and one becoming more acute as racing becomes more international, is that two horses from different countries can be given the same name. In Great Britain, the names of horses born overseas carry a suffix to indicate their country of foaling. Thus Swain (IRE), Peintre Celebre (USA), High-Rise (IRE). In the normal course of events these suffixes do not matter, but it can happen that two horses with the same name line up for the same race. In August 1979 Ginistrelli (USA) won a maiden race at Yarmouth, with Ginistrelli fourth; and in June 1994 the same course saw Averti (IRE) and Averti (USA) both running unplaced in the same race.

All these names, of course, have to be uttered, by the commentators if no one else, which brings us to the sometimes thorny issue of pronunciation. On the morning of the 1998 Murphy's Gold Cup the Cheltenham press room saw an arcane discussion between three distinguished callers of horses: Mike Cattermole, course commentator that day, Channel Four Racing's own Graham Goode, and the undisputed doyen of them all, Sir Peter O'Sullevan. The point under discussion was the correct way to pronounce the name of a fancied runner in the big race, Dr Leunt. Should it be 'Lunt', 'Learnt', 'Loont' or 'Loint' . . .?

Periodically, Weatherbys sends commentators guidance on the correct pronunciation (and meaning) of names, as advised by the horses' owners. The 1997 version contained such entries as:

Amlwch	Mmlook
An Seabhac	An Shawack (means: the hawk)
Aonfocaleile	Ane Foco Ella (means: any other word)
Dim Ots	Dim Ots (means: doesn't matter)
Ei Ei	Ee Ee
Facile Tigre	Faseel Teagrey
Fa-Eq	Far Eck (means: awake)
Geimhriuil	Gevrool (means: wintry)
Nicanjon	Nick and John
Tsessebe Hill	Tessa B Hill (Tsessebe is an antelope in Botswana)
Tui	Too Ee

You will not need reminding that the last one, Tui, is the Maori word for blackbird, but the list highlights the commentator's recurring pronunciation nightmare: Gaelic. Over the years dozens of horses bred in Ireland have been given Gaelic names, producing all sorts of headaches not only for race-callers but for those more intimately associated with the horses in question: that fine chaser Lean Ar Aghaidh was known in Stan Mellor's stable – and eventually to his admiring public – as 'Lean On The Aga'.

Trouble with those Gaelic names, of course, is spelling them right, and slips are made. The Toiseach, trained by James Fanshawe, was a leading fancy for the 1998 Hennessy Gold Cup at Newbury. The correct spelling of the office of prime minister of Ireland is the Taoiseach; might the horse have run better had he been spelt better?

How much simpler to be able to revert to the habit of most racing stables, where for day-to-day use the inmates are known not by their racing names but by much more familiar and easy appellations: for example, Reference Point, winner of the Derby, King George and St Leger in 1987, was known in Henry Cecil's yard as 'Herbie'. One Man was 'Solo'; Earth Summit is 'Digger'.

The Arab names beginning with 'Mu' pose a different sort of problem for racing followers – one not of pronunciation but of the ripe possibilities for confusion. Five consecutive entries in Timeform's *Racehorses of 1990*, for instance, cover Mujaazif, Mujadil, Mujtahid, Mukaddamah and Mukddaam, all owned by Sheikh Hamdan Al Maktoum, and two years later Muharib, Muhayaa, Muhit, Muhtarram, Muhtashim, Mujaazafah, Mujadil, Mujawab, Mujib, Mukaddamah and Muktaar all ran on the Flat in Britain. Fast forward a few years and things get no easier: Mutaahab, Mutaakkid, Mutabari, Mutabassir, Mutadarra, Mu-Tadil, Mutafarij, Mutafaweq, Mutahadeth, Mutamakin, Mutamam, Mutamayyaz, Mutasawwar, Mutawwaj and Mutazz all ran on the Flat in 1998.

Arkle to Aa-Youknownothing

Now, after all the rules, regulations and complications, a quick dip into the weird and wonderful world of horses' names . . .

- Arkle was named after a mountain overlooking the Scottish estate of his owner Anne, Duchess of Westminster. Another of the Duchess's fine chasers trained by Tom Dreaper was Ben Stack, also named after a mountain near the estate.

- Among other well-known chasers, The Dikler was named after a stream in Gloucestershire . . . Rubstic was named after the Swedish equivalent of the Brillo Pad . . . Garrison Savannah is the name of the racecourse in Barbados . . . Aldaniti was named after the four grandchildren of his breeder Tommy Barron: Alastair, David, Nicola and Timothy . . . But comedian Freddie Starr's post-Grand National assertion that Miinnehoma is Gaelic for 'lick my bollocks' can be put down to the euphoria of victory.

- Of notable performers on the Flat, Mill Reef was named after a part of the coast near the Antigua home of his owner Paul Mellon, and Mill Reef's son Shirley Heights after another feature of that Caribbean island . . . Lammtarra is the Arabic word for 'invisible' . . . Dr Devious was the nickname of the famous Irish vet Demi O'Byrne, who picked out the colt for Robert Sangster at the sales . . . Henbit is a sort of nettle . . . Blushing Groom was by Red God out of Runaway Bride, and Polish Precedent by Danzig out of Past Example.

- TV personality Katie Boyle is responsible for the 'friendly' theme in the naming of horses belonging to Peter (now Sir Peter) O'Sullevan. When her late husband Greville Baylis gave her a yearling colt, she told him: 'You want him to be fast, I just want him to be friendly.' So the colt was called Fast And Friendly, and when their friend O'Sullevan heard how this name had come about, he called his next horse Just Friendly – soon to be followed by such horses as Friendly Again and the great sprinter Be Friendly. O'Sullevan's other famous horse, Attivo, should have been named Amigo: the name had been reserved, but when it came to attaching name to horse, Weatherbys had let it go elsewhere. It was O'Sullevan's wife Pat who suggested Attivo – Italian for 'active' – for the agile colt, who went on to win the Triumph Hurdle and Chester Cup.

- Sir Clement Freud named a horse Weareagrandmother after Margaret Thatcher's famous pronouncement on the steps of 10 Downing Street as she displayed her first grandchild to the world's press.

- While some names suggest grandeur and aspiration, others are more downbeat. A horse name Toilet was unplaced in the race at Leicester in 1921 in which the great jockey Gordon Richards rode his first winner on Gay Lord . . . A horse glorying in the name Keith's Fridge raced in the 1970s . . . The Pub ran in a novice hurdle at Sedgefield in January 1996 . . . Grunge was in training with David Murray Smith in 1998 . . . Richard Hannon trained Sid in the early 1970s, while Eric was a good stayer who won the Chester Cup in 1972 . . . Sean, trained by Fred Rimell, won the Free Handicap Hurdle at Chepstow in 1978.

- Some horses are more cleverly named than might at first appear the case. The great miler Kris was by Sharpen Up out of Doubly Sure: a 'kris' is a double-edged Malaysian dagger. Kris's full brother Diesis, who won both the Middle Park Stakes and Dewhurst Stakes in 1982, was also very wittily named: a diesis is the double-dagger sign used in printing.

- Occasionally names seem to express frustration or indecision on the part of owners. Horses called Callitwhatyouwant and Itsnotnamedyet were in training in 1998.

- A horse cannot be renamed after being entered for a race, but until that stage names can be changed. Cacoethes, third to Nashwan in the 1989 Derby and a narrow runner-up to the same horse in that year's King George at Ascot, was bred in the United States and there given the name Our Friend Elvis. This was changed to the somewhat more elegant Cacoethes when the horse came to Britain.

- Amron, a sprinter trained by Jack Berry a few years back, was named after owner Roy Peebles's wife Norma.

- The late Charles St George named many of his horses after well-known artists, among them Giacometti and Lorenzaccio. His horse Peter Davies, winner of the William Hill Futurity in 1990, was named after St George's friend of the same name, who attracted something of a camp following when interviewed on Channel Four Racing. In 1978 St George had a top-notch two-year-old named R. B. Chesne in honour of the colt's co-owner, a Californian heart specialist.

- Robert Sangster, too, often names his horses after friends. For example, Commander Collins and Colonel Collins both acknowledge Tony Collins, the former trainer best known for his part in the famous Gay Future coup of

1974. Another of Sangster's well-known horses, Rodrigo de Triano, took his name from the lookout on Christopher Columbus's ship in 1492.

- The naming of American Pie, a mare in training in 1998 with Venetia Williams, is a poignant reminder of her breeder, the late jump jockey Richard Davis, who was killed in a fall at Southwell in 1996. 'American Pie' by Don McLean was Richard Davis's favourite song.

- The names of many horses in the great dynasty founded by Northern Dancer (himself by Native Dancer) perpetuate the theme of the theatre and dancing. Nijinsky and Nureyev are sons of Northern Dancer, as is Sadler's Wells, now the most influential sire in the world. Another generation on, the names of many of Sadler's Wells' offspring continue the theatrical connection: In The Wings, Entrepreneur, Opera House, King's Theatre, Royal Ballerina, Carnegie, French Ballerina, Theatreworld. Singspiel is by In The Wings out of Glorious Song: a *Singspiel* is a sort of opera which combines song and dialogue.

- Fortytwo Dee, a jumper with Tony Carroll, is owned by the bra manufacturer Triumph International. Her sire is Amazing Bust.

- The name of the colt Aa-Youknownothing, a winning two-year-old in 1998, reflects an exchange during the High Court case early that year when Jack and Lynda Ramsden and Kieren Fallon successfully fought a libel action against the *Sporting Life*. One of the key witnesses for the defence was *Raceform* race-reader Alan Amies, at whom the 'You know nothing' jibe was aimed by opposing barrister Patrick Milmo QC.

- One of the most curiously named horses of recent memory has been W Six Times, a good chaser trained by

Michael Dickinson in the 1980s. The name derives from the form-book assessment: 'Waited with, will win when wanted'.

- Strong Arab influence is widespread in the naming of horses, not least in the use of 'Bint' – as in Bint Salsabil or Bint Shadayid. 'Bint' is Arabic for 'daughter of'.

- Her Majesty the Queen has a reputation for naming her horses with particular wit and ingenuity. Here are a few examples from the royal string:

  > Mister Glum by Ron's Victory out of Australia Fair
  > Arabian Story by Sharrood out of Once Upon A Time
  > Rash Gift by Cadeaux Genereux out of Nettle
  > Whitechapel by Arctic Tern out of Christchurch
  > Feel Free by Generous out of As You Desire Me.

- Until 1946 a horse could race unnamed, in which case it would be identified by the name of its dam: thus the first race at Newmarket on Two Thousand Guineas day 1945 was won by a filly described in the form book as 'Ling f.'– her dam being the mare Ling.

- The 1812 Two Thousand Guineas was won by a horse named Cwrw – the only winner of an English Classic whose name contained no vowels.

- You do not have to own a horse to register a name. Weatherbys will reserve a name for you against the moment when you have a horse to bear it.

- The great American horse Cigar (see page 113) takes his name from an aircraft checkpoint in the Gulf of Mexico.

- A few tasty Classic winners: Olive (1814 Two Thousand Guineas), Pastille (1822 Oaks), Mayonaise (1859 One Thousand Guineas), Mincemeat (1864 Oaks), Mincepie

(1856 Oaks), Macaroni (1863 Two Thousand Guineas and Derby), Tomato (1864 One Thousand Guineas), Persimmon (1896 Derby), Spearmint (1906 Derby), Manna (1925 Two Thousand Guineas and Derby) and Sandwich (1931 St Leger). Less palatably, the 1890 One Thousand Guineas was won by Semolina, and the 1843 Oaks by Poison.

• And finally, no foray into the matter of racehorses' name is ever complete without mention of Kybo, winner of the Christmas Hurdle at Kempton in 1978 and owned by Isidore Kerman. When Kerman was away at boarding school his mother would send him letters which ended with the instruction KYBO – maternal shorthand for 'Keep Your Bowels Open'.

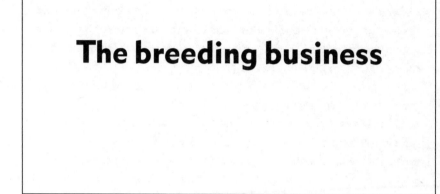

The breeding business

HORSE SENSE from Lesley Graham

I spend a lot of time at the yearling sales analysing my likes and dislikes in an individual. Flat horses are, of course, relatively immature, but I like a horse to have a nice eye (and therefore a good attitude) and an athletic walk. If an individual uses himself well in his slower paces he stands a better chance of generating greater momentum when going up a gear.

Some horses truly 'fill the eye', and generally they have substance, good depth and quarters, and a presence. For me on the Flat this was best achieved by Nashwan – although of the horses I have bought, I fell for Crumpton Hill on sight, enough to forgive him bad front legs – and over the jumps I loved Bradbury Star.

The breeding business

The Thoroughbred racehorse is a very specialised animal, carefully bred for a particular purpose – to win races. But the apparently straightforward requirement to breed a horse which can run fast has to be balanced by other considerations, such as soundness (a horse which keeps breaking down under the pressures of training and racing is not much of a prospect) and temperament (a horse not mentally equipped to cope with the strain of racing will not perform to the best of its physical ability).

The evolution of the breed

The racehorse we know today is the result of some three centuries of careful breeding. By the sixteenth century the type of horse most commonly used for racing in what is now the British Isles was the 'hobby', a small but extremely tough and durable animal which had been imported from Spain to Ireland, whence it had become popular for racing in England. But the desire to add more speed to the bloodlines led, towards the end of the seventeenth century, to the import from the Near East of the three famous Arab stallions whose influence has made the English Thoroughbred the standard breed for the sport in all major racing countries of the world. Every single modern Thoroughbred traces his or her ancestry to one of this historic trio:

- The Byerley Turk, foaled around 1680, who had supposedly seen action at the Battle of the Boyne before being sent
to stud in County Durham. Among his distinguished
descendants is The Tetrarch, 'The Spotted Wonder', who
was unbeaten in seven races as a two-year-old in 1913 and
was probably one of the fastest horses of all time, and –
rather more recently – Derby winners such as Blakeney
and Dr Devious.
- The Darley Arabian, foaled in 1700 and sent to England as
a four-year-old. He is the progenitor of the vast majority of
modern Thoroughbreds, and many of the most powerful
bloodlines of the twentieth century are offshoots of his,
notably that of Northern Dancer, sire of Nijinsky, Sadler's
Wells and many other famous racehorses.
- The Godolphin Arabian, foaled in 1724 and (according to
some accounts) discovered in Paris pulling a water cart. He
is the direct ancestor of 1964 Derby winner Santa Claus,
and of the famous American horse foaled in 1917, Man
O'War.

The importance of these three is as stallions rather than as racehorses
– none of them ever seems to have taken part in a race – but it was not
long before their influence on the racing scene became very marked. The
Darley Arabian's son Flying Childers, foaled in 1714, is held to be the
first truly great English racehorse despite running in only two races, and
Flying Childers' full brother Bartlett's Childers was great-grandsire of
Eclipse (see page 122).

Another famous horse from the eighteenth century whose name lives
on is Gimcrack, foaled in 1760. He raced between 1764 and 1771,
winning twenty-six of the thirty-six races in which he took part. In
1766 Gimcrack raced in France in a 'time trial', covering twenty-two
and a half miles in an hour. But he was beaten on the two occasions he
ran at York – somewhat ironically, in view of the fact that he is now
commemorated there in the great two-year-old race at the August
Meeting.

The races which horses such as Eclipse or Gimcrack contested
would not for the most part have been the kind of events familiar to
today's racegoers. Horse races in the eighteenth century were usually

run over what we would consider exceptionally long distances (around four miles) and in heats: the winners would go through to run off for the prize. But towards the end of the century significant changes took place. Races for two-year-olds were instituted, encouraging breeders to produce more precocious types rather than solely horses who would not run until they were mature at four or five. Handicaps were introduced, to make racing a more interesting betting medium. And what became the Classics, for three-year-olds only, were first staged: the St Leger in 1776, the Oaks in 1779 and the Derby in 1780. (The Two Thousand Guineas was first run early the following century, in 1809, with the inaugural One Thousand five years later in 1814.)

Shorter races called for horses who could run faster, and there was more emphasis on early development. Racehorses became bigger. The Darley Arabian had stood fifteen hands high, the Godolphin Arabian just fourteen hands three inches and the diminutive Gimcrack fourteen hands one inch; Eclipse, at fifteen hands three inches, was considered tall. By the middle of the nineteenth century the average Thoroughbred was about six inches taller than the founding fathers of the breed.

Since the Second World War the increasing importance and influence of American bloodlines have seen the ideal middle distance of the Classic horse on the Flat shift from a mile and a half (the distance of the Derby at Epsom) to a mile and a quarter (the distance of the Kentucky Derby): connections of a potential stallion looking to attract US breeders will want their horse to have won over ten furlongs if possible. Another recent trend which has been widely approved of by racing enthusiasts is a move away from extreme precocity towards a longer racing career for the best horses (see pages 24–5). It is no longer crucial for a Derby candidate to have shown serious form as a two-year-old – 1993 winner Commander In Chief did not race at all as a juvenile, and of Derby winners in the 1990s, only Generous and Dr Devious won Group One races at two.

Horses bred for National Hunt racing are given more time to mature before being subjected to the rigours of racing. The earliest age at which a horse may run over hurdles is three, and many a potential steeplechaser is kept as a 'store', not going into training until the age of four or five.

The big players

Nowadays the higher reaches of the bloodstock business may seem to those pressing their noses against the glass the private province of a few very rich men, with Flat racing dominated at the very highest level by two camps:

- In the left corner, the Maktoum family from Dubai. The four Maktoum brothers – Sheikh Mohammed bin Rashid Al Maktoum, Sheikh Hamdan Al Maktoum, Sheikh Maktoum Al Maktoum and Sheikh Ahmed Al Maktoum – have long been pre-eminent figures in European racing and latterly have extended their reach worldwide, owning among them a glittering array of top racehorses and each developing extensive breeding operations (see page 69 below). But Maktoum influence increased even further with the establishment of the Godolphin operation – brainchild of Sheikh Mohammed – an innovative project, producing its first runners in 1994, in which top horses are sent to winter in the warmth of Dubai before being returned to the Godolphin yard in Newmarket for the British Flat season. (Godolphin's investment in buying the defunct French racecourse Evry as a base from 1999 for its two-year-olds, where they will be placed in the charge of leading young trainer David Loder, is another sign of its commitment.) The Maktoums are very big players at the top yearling sales, where they often come head-to-head in the bidding stakes with . . .
- In the right corner, a group of high-rolling owner–breeders centred around the Coolmore Stud in Tipperary (see page 69), of whom the most public faces are Michael Tabor, in whose colours such horses as 1997 Two Thousand Guineas winner Entrepreneur have had moments of glory, and John Magnier. Many of their horses – for example, 1998 Two Thousand Guineas winner King Of Kings – are trained by Aidan O'Brien at Ballydoyle, former base of the legendary Irish trainer Vincent O'Brien (no relation).

The results of the 1998 English Classics displayed the domination of the Maktoum and O'Brien camps:

- Two Thousand Guineas winner King Of Kings, trained by Aidan O'Brien, ran in the colours of Mrs Susan Magnier (wife of John).
- One Thousand Guineas winner Cape Verdi ran under the Godolphin banner.
- Oaks winner Shahtoush was trained by Aidan O'Brien.
- Derby winner High-Rise was owned by Sheikh Mohammed Obaid Al-Maktoum, cousin of 'the' Sheikh Mohammed; later in the season it was announced that High-Rise would transfer from trainer Luca Cumani to the Godolphin operation for his 1999 campaign.
- St Leger winner Nedawi ran under the Godolphin banner.

Other owner–breeders who have been operating on a very large scale for many years include Khalid Abdullah (owner of such horses as Dancing Brave – see page 115 – and Zafonic as well as Derby winners Quest For Fame and Commander In Chief), the Aga Khan (owner of Shergar and Shahrastani) and Prince Fahd Salman (owner of Generous), while comparatively new kids on the block include The Thoroughbred Corporation, the racing and breeding operation of Saudi prince Ahmed bin Salman, whose well-known horses have included Royal Anthem and Killer Instinct.

These are some of the major players; but breeding racehorses is still much more than a private playground for the super-rich. The history of National Hunt racing is littered with examples of cheaply bred horses who have hit the heights on the racecourse. The rags-to-riches story of Red Rum is told on pages 134–6, and Desert Orchid was home-bred by James Burridge from a mare whose dam he had purchased for 175 guineas.

All in the genes

At whatever level, the real fascination of breeding is in the choice of mating, as enthralling and unpredictable in horses as it can be in humans.

All sorts of theories have been tried out in the quest for the perfect racehorse. If the simplest is the notion of mating the best with the best to produce the best, the most romantic has to be the story of Signorinetta. In 1904 her owner Chevalier Ginistrelli had put her dam Signorina to her sire Chaleureux because the two horses had struck up a relationship during the sire's morning walk past the dam's paddock in Newmarket. Chaleureux was a very humble sire but Ginistrelli, struck by how the two horses were attached by, as he put it, 'the boundless laws of sympathy and love', decided to take a chance. Call him an old softy – but the offspring Signorinetta won the 1908 Derby at 100–1, and, for good measure, the Oaks two days later.

But romance rarely enters into racehorse breeding, and a more realistic approach is that of the late John Hislop, breeder of the great Brigadier Gerard (see page 109): 'All that the breeder can do is to try to arrange matters so that there is a reasonable chance of the right genetic shakeup emerging, and hope for the best.'

The 'right genetic shakeup' would be a balance of temperamental and physical attributes that embodied speed, stamina, toughness, conformation and resolution in their ideal proportions. Many breeders seek this grail of their art through inbreeding (choosing a match in which a particular horse or family of horses appears on both sides of the pedigree) in order to strengthen some chosen feature. Thus Dream Well, winner of the Prix du Jockey-Club and Irish Derby in 1998, is inbred 2 x 4 to Northern Dancer: that is, Northern Dancer appears both in the second generation of Dream Well's pedigree as sire of his sire Sadler's Wells, and in the fourth generation on the other side as sire of Northfields, grandsire of Dream Well's dam.

The opposite of inbreeding is outcrossing, where the parents do not have ancestors in common in their recent pedigree. Such notable 1998 performers as High-Rise, Commander Collins, Silver Patriarch and Sagamix have no duplications within five generations.

A 'nick' in breeding jargon is when two specific unrelated families consistently produce a successful outcome.

The mating game

Breeding on an international scale is an immensely complex business, but the fundamental cycle of the breeding year in Britain is fairly straightforward. On 15 February begins the 'covering season', which lasts five months until 15 July. The owner of the mare will have decided, usually after much research, advice and pondering, which stallion he wishes to mate her with. Major breeders may send a mare to a stallion whom they themselves own or in whom they have an interest, but in any event the stallion will normally be standing at a stud, to which the mare will be sent. The gestation period of a Thoroughbred being about eleven months (320–360 days), she may well be carrying a foal conceived the previous year; in this case she will arrive shortly before that foal is due, give birth at the stud and then await the next covering. She will come into season ('on heat') about eight to ten days after foaling, and thereafter at three-weekly intervals.

If the mare appears to be in season, the next stage is to introduce her to a 'teaser', a stallion – in some cases, but not all, sterile – kept by the stud for the purpose of gauging the mares' sexual response. The teaser flirts with the mare by nibbling her across the 'trying board' over which they are introduced, and if she reacts favourably he is led away to repeat this frustrating task with another mare while the vet examines this one. The reason why the stallion who will actually cover the mare is not allowed to engage in this foreplay himself is to protect him – and his owners' investment: for if the mare is not receptive she may show her reluctance with considerable violence, and a swift bite or kick could cause considerable damage to millions of pounds' worth of horseflesh. Some stallions, moreover, can do with a warm-up act, being less than entirely psychologically committed or biologically suited to their calling: The Tetrarch, one of the most brilliant racehorses the Turf has ever seen, had a singular lack of interest in sex while at stud, though he managed to produce several good offspring, and more recently the stud career of the great American horse Cigar (see page 114) was a disaster: he proved infertile, and was taken out of stud duties.

As for the teaser, just occasionally he gets a piece of the action for himself. In 1986 the broodmare Branitska, due to be covered by Wolver Heights at the Stetchworth Stud in Newmarket, declined to cooperate. 'Branitska just would not take to Wolver Heights at all,' recalled stud owner Bill Gredley, 'and kicked him like mad. In the end we brought the teaser forward, and because she stood still for him we thought, "Why not?"' The offspring, well named Call To Arms, was beaten a neck at 66–1 in the 1989 Dewhurst Stakes.

If the mare's reactions to the teaser show that the time is right for the covering to go ahead, she is washed off in the appropriate area (to prevent the spread of infection), her tail is bandaged and she is fitted with felt shoes on her hind feet in case she should lash out. The stallion is then led into the covering barn to meet his mate. One groom holds the mare's upper lip in a twitch (a loop of rope attached to a stick) to keep her still while another lifts one of her forelegs to make it difficult for her to kick out. He releases it as she is mounted, when the stallion man, who looks after the stallion and supervises the mating, helps his charge achieve efficient penetration. The whole covering operation should take a minute or two.

If the mare does not conceive at that covering, the procedure is repeated when she returns in season, and a stallion will sometimes cover the same mare several times. (He will often need to cover several mares in a day, as it cannot be accurately predicted well in advance exactly when any mare will be receptive.) Although a pregnancy can be detected as early as fourteen days after covering, the mare will not normally return to her owner until the pregnancy has become properly established, around two months after covering. She will then remain at home while the foal develops, returning to the stud the following year in time to give birth.

Covering fees for stallions vary considerably according to the status of the stallion involved. Nominations (a nomination being the right to send a mare to be covered by a particular stallion) to Sadler's Wells, currently the most influential stallion in the world, are not available to any Tom, Dick or Harry breeder, but had you set your sights a little lower for the 1998 covering season you could, subject to availability and the acceptability of your mare, have had her covered by

- Benny The Dip, 1997 Derby winner, for US$25,000 at Claiborne Farm, Kentucky;
- In The Wings, winner of the 1990 Coronation Cup and Breeders' Cup Turf, for £IR15,000 at the Kildangan Stud, County Kildare;
- Celtic Swing, outstanding two-year-old in 1994 and Prix du Jockey-Club hero in 1995, for £6,500 at the National Stud in Newmarket.

There is usually a 'no foal, no fee' condition which stipulates that the fee is payable only if the mare is certified in foal on 1 October of the year in which the covering took place. Sometimes other arrangements apply, under which, for example, the breeder pays half the fee at covering and half when conception is confirmed, or part of the fee is held back until a live foal is born.

The very best male racehorses are often 'syndicated' for stud purposes, which means that ownership is divided into shares (normally forty), each worth an equal portion of the total valuation of the horse. For example, Dancing Brave (see page 115) was initially syndicated in forty shares costing £350,000 each, putting a total valuation on the horse of £14 million.

The owners of top stallions usually put a ceiling on the number of mares their prized investment may cover in a season – not because of the risk of exhaustion to the horse but on the grounds that too many offspring would undermine the value of the stock. Other stallions have had to be more vigorous: Be My Native, winner of the Coronation Cup in 1983, covered 325 mares at the Grange Stud in County Cork during 1994, and it is common for National Hunt sires to be kept very busy.

Young hopefuls

When to have a mare covered, and thus when her foal is to be born, can be a difficult question. A foal conceived at a covering in March should be born the following February, whereas a June mating would mean (assuming a full-term pregnancy) a May foal. Taking into account the rule by which every Thoroughbred's official birthday falls on the 1 January preceding its biological birthday, deciding on the ideal timing involves weighing up different factors: an early foal may mature sooner than others of its generation, and thus possibly have the advantage over them in juvenile races; but a later foal will have the benefit of better grass and climate when it is very young, which may give its physical development a better start.

The 1 January birthday also has the potential to scupper a racing career before the potential performer has so much as got to its feet. One mating when the timing nearly went spectacularly wrong concerned two very well-known names. On New Year's Day 1992 Salsabil, brilliant winner of the One Thousand Guineas, Oaks and Irish Derby in 1990, gave birth to a filly foal by 1989 Two Thousand Guineas and Derby winner Nashwan. Had that foal been born a day earlier she would have officially become a yearling on 1 January when in reality just a single day old, and thus – despite Mum and Dad having won five Classics between them – not much of a racing proposition.

A commercial breeder may sell the foal later in the year of its birth, or may wait until the following year, when the youngster will be sold as a yearling and go into training with a view to racing on the Flat the year after as a two-year-old. The business of buying foals and then selling them on as yearlings is known as 'pinhooking' and can be very profitable, as it cuts out the costs of breeding and of keeping the pregnant mare: the most notable horse of recent years to have been pinhooked was the 1991 Derby winner Generous, sold for 80,000 Irish guineas at the Goffs' December Sales as a foal in 1988 and then sold on as a yearling in 1989 for 200,000 Irish guineas.

The top yearling sales, where trainers, owners and bloodstock agents compete at auction for the best young horses, form a great international circus, starting at the Keeneland sales in Kentucky in July, moving on to Deauville in France and the Goffs' sales in Ireland, and culminating in the October sales held at Newmarket by the famous firm of Tattersalls, founded in 1766 and the world's most renowned bloodstock auctioneers.

The competition in these contests for the Classic winners of the future can be extremely hot, and periodically (especially when fuelled by a head-to-head battle between two or more of the dominant players) sends prices sky-high. In recent years the market has settled down somewhat, with the realisation that yearling prices were bearing little relation to the likely returns from either racing or breeding; but back in the mid-1980s the hothouse atmosphere of the sale ring saw some crazy sums changing hands. The current record price paid for a yearling at the sales was set when Seattle Dancer – a son of Nijinsky – was sold to the Robert Sangster group of breeders for $13.1 million in 1985. The colt turned out to be a reasonably good racehorse, but – hardly surprisingly, set such a target – recouped only a small portion of his purchase price in prize money on the track.

Even that could not be said of the famous Snaafi Dancer, the Northern Dancer colt who caused a sensation when sold to Sheikh Mohammed at

Tattersalls Houghton Sale, Newmarket 1998

A measure of the current state of the top end of the bloodstock market can be gauged from the bare statistics of Britain's most prestigious yearling sale in September/October 1998. (Note: a guinea, the currency in which bloodstock sales are still conducted in Great Britain and Ireland, is £1.05.)

- 224 yearlings were offered for sale, of which 207 were sold;
- aggregate price of those sold was 35,471,000 guineas;
- average price was 171,357 guineas (in 1997 it was 105,998);
- median price – the halfway point in the range of selling prices, with as many above as below – was 100,000 guineas (1997: 80,000 guineas);
- top price was 3 million guineas – a European record for a yearling – for a colt by Nureyev;
- two other yearlings made seven figures: a colt by Rainbow Quest selling for 2.2 million guineas and a colt by Sadler's Wells for 1 million guineas.

the Keeneland sales in 1983 for $10.2 million (then the world record price) after a prolonged sale-ring battle with Sangster. Snaafi Dancer went into training with John Dunlop, where it rapidly became apparent that, as a racehorse, he was completely useless. He then was shipped off to stud in Canada, where he proved equally useless as a stallion.

Although the yearling sales attract the most attention and publicity, other Thoroughbreds pass through the ring – foals, broodmares and horses in training being the main types. The sale of Gatflax for 200,000 guineas in 1998 set a new record for a jumper in training.

The great studs

Studs are the factories of the bloodstock business, with some 300 stud farms producing the 5,000 or so Thoroughbred foals born in Britain every year. They range from the huge establishments of the super-rich owner–breeders to working farms where the owner will keep a mare or two and breed for fun. Many studs do not stand stallions but only house mares.

The National Stud

Spreading today across a 500-acre site beside the July Course at Newmarket, the National Stud has over the twentieth century been home to some of the best stallions in British bloodstock history. One of the few studs which is open to the public on a regular basis, it was founded in 1916, when Colonel Hall-Walker, later Lord Wavertree, presented his bloodstock and sold his stud in Ireland to the nation. (That establishment, just outside Kildare, is now the Irish National Stud.) In 1943 the National Stud's bloodstock was moved to Gillingham in Dorset, and after the war to a second location in West Grinstead: it was here that the great Italian horse Ribot (see page 137) was born. In the early 1960s it was decided to concentrate on standing high-class stallions; a new stud was built in Newmarket, and its first stallions moved in during 1966.

Through great stallions such as Blandford, Big Game, Never Say Die and Mill Reef, the John Skeaping statue of whom graces the Stud's grounds, the National Stud has exerted a considerable influence on racing the world over. With the growing domination of Arab, American and Japanese breeders it has not been possible for the Stud to sustain that influence, but it still boasts a fine roster of stallions: those on duty in 1999 include Air Express, Hector Protector and 1996 Derby winner Shaamit.

The Royal Studs

The Royal Studs in Sandringham – owned by the Crown – have a long and distinguished history: Royal Applause is now the principal stallion here, the studs' two outstanding sires Shirley Heights and Bustino having both died in 1997.

The Arab studs

The Maktoum family has gone into the Thoroughbred breeding business with the depth of enthusiasm and pockets with which they took up racing, and many of the major studs in Britain and Ireland now represent the breeding end of the brothers' racing operations.

Sheikh Mohammed's flagship stud is Dalham Hall near Newmarket, home to an illustrious sequence of top-class stallions: Dancing Brave began his stud career here before being exported to Japan. The roster of stallions at Dalham Hall in 1998 featured such familiar names as Halling, Lion Cavern, Machiavellian, Mark Of Esteem, Mtoto, Polish Precedent, Shareef Dancer and Singspiel. The Sheikh's principal stud in Ireland is Kildangan, in County Kildare, home of stallions In The Wings, Lycius and Pennekamp.

Hamdan Al Maktoum's breeding operation is run under the banner of the Shadwell Stud, based at Thetford in Norfolk and boasting the services of Nashwan and Green Desert; another flagship of this operation is the Derrinstown Stud in County Maynooth. The eldest of the brothers, Maktoum Al Maktoum, has the Gainsborough Stud in Berkshire, and the youngest, Ahmed Al Maktoum, owns the Aston Upthorpe Stud at Aston Tirrold in Oxfordshire.

Khalid Abdullah's bloodstock interests are conducted under the banner of Juddmonte Farms; his Banstead Manor Stud near Newmarket is the home of stallions Rainbow Quest and Zafonic.

Coolmore

The Coolmore Stud, near Fethard in County Tipperary, Ireland, is the largest stallion station in Europe. The stallions serving mares here and at related studs in the same ownership include the likes of Alzao, Fairy King, Be My Guest and more recent arrivals such as Entrepreneur and Peintre Celebre, with in undisputed pride of place the great Sadler's Wells.

A measure of the excellence of Coolmore as a breeding establishment is the sheer quality of horses conceived here. In the list of stallions who produced the most winners of Pattern races in Europe in 1998, Coolmore fills the top four spots with:

- Sadler's Wells: winners of fifteen pattern races, including Commander Collins, Dream Well (twice), Kayf Tara (twice), King Of Kings, Leggera (twice) and Sea Wave;

- Alzao: winners of eleven Pattern races, including Alborada (three Group wins), Winona and Shahtoush;
- Fairy King: winners of eleven Pattern races, including Second Empire and Victory Note (twice);
- Danehill: winners of ten Pattern races, including Wannabe Grand (twice).

Another mark of the pre-eminence of Coolmore is the fact that the winners of the first four English Classics in 1998 were all sired by stallions standing at the stud: King Of Kings (by Sadler's Wells), Cape Verdi (by the late Caerleon), Shahtoush (by Alzao) and High-Rise (by High Estate, who had been at Coolmore until being exported to Japan in 1996).

Sadler's Wells

A son of Northern Dancer, Sadler's Wells was a very good racehorse owned by Robert Sangster and trained by Vincent O'Brien, under whose care he won in 1984 the Irish Two Thousand Guineas, Eclipse Stakes (beating Time Charter) and Phoenix Champion Stakes. Retiring to the Coolmore Stud at the end of that year, he soon established himself as the most important sire in the world, and has been champion sire in Great Britain every year from 1990 to the present with the exception of 1991 (when another Coolmore resident Caerleon took the title, mainly thanks to the exploits of his son Generous). Among Sadler's Wells' offspring are:

- Old Vic, winner of the Prix du Jockey-Club and Irish Derby in 1989;
- Salsabil, winner of the One Thousand Guineas, Oaks and Irish Derby in 1990;
- Opera House, winner of the Coronation Cup, Eclipse and King George in 1993;
- top hurdlers Istabraq and Pridwell; and
- countless other star performers such as Entrepreneur, King Of Kings, Dream Well, King's Theatre, Intrepidity, Barathea, Carnegie, Moonshell, In The Wings, Leggera . . .

Studs in America

In the United States, with its Thoroughbred population of over half a million horses, breeding for racing is big business: some 50,000 Thoroughbred foals are registered every year.

While every state of the union has some interest in the Thoroughbred, the spiritual home of racing in the United States is Kentucky, where most of the famous American studs are located. Claiborne Farm, near the town of Paris, has been the home of some of the most notable horses of recent times, including Secretariat (see page 144) and Derby winners Sir Ivor and Nijinsky: it was to Claiborne that 1997 Derby winner Benny The Dip retired to take up breeding duties – and, on an unhappier note, here that the great mare Triptych met her untimely end after a night-time collision with a truck in 1989.

Other famous Kentucky studs include Gainesway, Calumet, Spend-thrift, Ashford (part of the Coolmore Group) and Three Chimneys.

The other major Thoroughbred-breeding states are California, Maryland, New York and Florida, while Virginia is the home of Paul Mellon's Rokeby Farm and several other notable establishments. The most famous stud in Canada is Windfields Farm in Ontario, birthplace in 1967 of Nijinsky, winner of the English Triple Crown in 1970 and the last horse to perform that feat (see page 129).

Lammtarra was the first Derby winner to be the produce of a Derby winner and an Oaks winner. The 1995 Epsom hero was by Nijinsky, winner of the Derby in 1970, out of Snow Bride, promoted to first place in the 1989 Oaks on the disqualification of Aliysa for failing the dope test.

In training

HORSE SENSE from Simon Holt

For me, a racehorse's true quality is in his head, as much as in his legs. Not what's going on inside his head (not much, in the case of most horses!) but how the head is carried. For me a horse who gallops with his head down is invariably a trier, while one whose head is held high, with eyes to the sky, may well be the opposite. Jumpers like Pegwell Bay, Docklands Express, Viking Flagship and Celtic Shot were all head-down triers; more recently, on the Flat, Auction House is another good, honest example. Mind you, King Of Kings carried his head very high but it didn't stop him winning the Two Thousand Guineas!

In training

There are around 12,000 horses in training in Britain, spread around the country among some 700 trainers. But whether a horse is with one of the very big trainers – Henry Cecil or John Dunlop on the Flat, Martin Pipe or David Nicholson over jumps – or one of the small yards with just a handful of horses, the routine to which he will be subjected to get race-fit will follow a certain pattern.

Before racecourse action can be contemplated, however, the young horse must be given his all-important basic education.

First lessons

A yearling bought at the autumn sales and expected to run on the Flat as a two-year-old will go from the sales to the yard of his new trainer, where the process of breaking in will begin immediately. On the other hand, a horse who is to be kept as a 'store' for racing over jumps without racing on the Flat will probably not begin his first lessons until much later: Arkle was not broken in until he was nearly four.

Whenever it happens, breaking in – an unfortunate term for a process intended to imbue the young pupil with trust and compliance – tends to follow a certain pattern. The horse will have worn a halter or head collar and become accustomed to being led from his days as a very young foal and will be used to human company, but breaking in even a good-natured and well-handled youngster is both a tricky and a crucial operation, and for this reason is usually entrusted to a highly experienced stable lad. For the same reason the process cannot be rushed, normally taking two to three weeks.

Bitting to backing

First the horse must get used to the feel of a bit in his mouth. He is introduced to this peculiar sensation by means of a mouthing bit, with jangling 'keys' on the mouthpiece with which the youngster can fiddle with his tongue. This encourages the horse to produce saliva and to relax the jaw with the bit in his mouth, both conducive to the desirable 'soft' mouth, responsive to the rider's contact on the reins. At the next stage, long reins are attached to the bit on either side and the horse is taught to walk with the lad behind him; in this way the horse gets used to feeling the signals coming through the reins to his mouth. Then he learns to lunge – to walk and trot in circles on the end of a single long rein. In both long-reining and lungeing, the horse learns to respond to the voice of the handler as well as to pressure on his mouth through the reins and bit.

Once the horse is responding well to the signals he is receiving, he is introduced to the roller, a padded girth fitted in the position where there will later be a saddle: the reins are fitted through rings on the roller to replicate the feel of the rider's hands on the reins. Next, the roller is replaced by a saddle, so that the horse can become accustomed to a larger item on his back. At each stage, with each new piece of unfamiliar equipment, the horse will continue to be lunged and long-reined to get him used to these strange sensations.

Eventually comes the big moment when the horse is 'backed' – introduced for the first time to a rider. Like everything else in breaking in, this is done in careful stages. First a lad will lean across the horse, then lay across his back for a few moments, then for longer – all the while making the horse amenable to the new sensations – and before long he will sit quietly and loosely astride. Then the horse will be lunged with the lad on top, and finally, when it is clear that the horse accepts the presence of the rider as normal, the lunge rein will be removed and the horse will be 'ridden away'. Now he must no longer look to instructions from the ground, but must obey the signals given from the saddle.

Restricted at first to quiet walking and trotting, the youngster will soon be got used to being ridden in company by engaging in a gentle canter up the gallops, usually with an older horse to show the way. (Viking Flagship, David Nicholson's great two-mile chaser, took on this educative role with the stable youngsters after his retirement from active service in 1998.)

That is the traditional way, but times are changing, and new methods of teaching a young horse are beginning to be more widely adopted – and, significantly, described as 'starting' rather than 'breaking'. These rely to a large extent on the work of Monty Roberts, the American guru of 'starting' horses who is often described as 'the original horse whisperer'. The key to Roberts's method has been to encourage rather than subordinate, to adopt a slow, softly-softly approach which gives the horse complete confidence, and, crucially, makes the horse come to the teacher, rather than have the teacher force his or her attentions on the horse.

Riding horse to racehorse

The first stages of breaking in, or starting, will be much the same for a horse destined for any equestrian discipline; but the potential racehorse must learn some very specific skills particular to his intended calling.

For a horse who will run on the Flat, there is the requirement of getting used to the starting stalls. Using a set of stalls kept for the purpose on the training grounds, the yearling is led quietly into the stalls with his rider, at first walking straight through and then pausing in the stall before walking, and then trotting, out when the front doors are opened. When he is used to that he will be ridden out of the stalls more forcefully and be allowed to canter for a few hundred yards.

On the Flat or over jumps, every racehorse must learn the art of keeping himself balanced while negotiating bends and how to stretch out at the gallop. It is not until these crucial stages are broached that the trainer will learn the potential racing ability of his charge.

Equipment

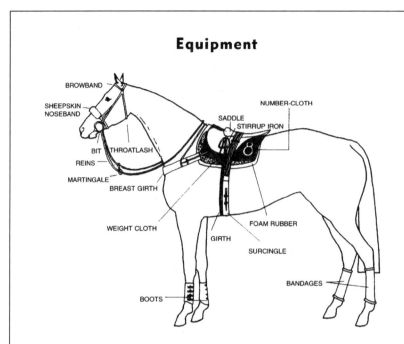

The bridle is usually made of leather, though in recent years many trainers have discovered that racing on all-weather surfaces has damaged the leather, and bridles made of synthetic materials are now a common sight on the all-weather tracks. Usually the part of the reins which the jockey holds is coated with rubber to improve grip.

There are several variations on the basic bridle. The sheepskin noseband theoretically encourages the horse to look further ahead, stretch out its feet and keep its head down, but often the fitting of one simply reflects stable preference. Other variations include the Australian cheeker – a rubber strip which runs from the browband down the centre of the horse's nose, dividing to be attached to each end of the bit, thus keeping the bit high in the horse's mouth – and the drop noseband, often fitted to help control a hard puller. Some trainers use the Grakle or cross noseband, which prevents the horse crossing its jaw, again giving extra control over a particularly keen horse.

The most common bit is the jointed 'snaffle': two lengths of metal joined in the middle and attached to rings at either end. A 'pricker' is a small brush-like device fitted to the outside of the bit which makes it uncomfortable for a horse to lean one way, and thus helps keep the wanderer straight. An alternative remedy sometimes used with a horse who tends to hang is a bit with cheekpieces - long pieces of metal at either end of the mouthpiece which lie alongside the horse's cheeks and prevent the bit being pulled through the mouth. A horse prone to 'swallow its tongue' (see page 93) may have the wayward organ restrained with a tonguestrap, which ties the tongue to the lower jaw.

A racing martingale consists of two small metal rings attached by a leather strip: this keeps the reins in place.

When saddling up a horse before a race, the trainer will usually place on his back: first, a sheet of foam rubber (or maybe a piece of chamois leather, less likely to slip); the weight-cloth (if necessary), a pad incorporating pockets into which are inserted thin strips of metal which bring the weight of jockey and equipment up to the required mark; the number-cloth; and the saddle itself. Although traditionally made of leather, racing saddles are nowadays also manufactured from synthetic materials in an attempt to reduce their weight. Most jockeys have several saddles, the choice of one for each individual race depending on the weight to be carried. The smallest might weigh as little as eight ounces in itself, though that weight will rise once the saddle is 'made up' with stirrup leathers, irons and girths.

The saddle is secured on the horse's back by means of a girth, buckled under the flaps on each side of the saddle, and by a surcingle, the additional strap which goes right round the horse's belly and over the top of the saddle. Extra security comes with a breast-girth (shown in the drawing) or breast-plate (straps attached to each side of the saddle and joined to the lowest point of the girth by another strap passing between the forelegs.

On the horse's legs leather boots or bandages are a common sight – especially with jumpers, for whom they offer protection from knocks and cuts when taking hurdles or fences.

Most racehorses are fitted with iron-based horseshoes at home, but these will be swapped for much lighter aluminium shoes (plates) when racing. The shoes are attached to the feet by thin nails driven (by the farrier) into the wall of the hoof. Horses with specially sensitive feet may wear stick-on shoes attached not by nails but by a strong glue.

A horse's vision is very unlike a human's, and fitting blinkers helps it concentrate during a race by fixing its vision on what is going on ahead. Horses wearing blinkers have traditionally been damned as 'rogues', but countless perfectly genuine horses have run well in them. It is always worth paying attention to the chances of a horse wearing blinkers for the first time, as they can bring about an extra-ordinary transformation in form. (Blinkers may come with a 'full cup' or – allowing more sideways vision – 'half cup'.)

A visor is a pair of blinkers with an aperture in each of the eyeshields to allow for a small amount of lateral vision, while a hood leaves the eyes clear but covers the ears. A horse with defective vision in one eye may be fitted with an eyecover, which covers the affected eye completely. Runners on all-weather surfaces are sometimes fitted with an eyeshield, with cups made of mesh or a transparent material which protects the horse's eyes from kickback.

Earplugs may be fitted on a horse susceptible to racecourse noise; one of the Jockey Club's more intriguing rules dictates that they may not be removed during a race.

Getting down to work

Having been broken in – or 'started' – the young Flat horse will commence his serious training in the spring of his two-year-old year, and once he has learned the rudiments of racing alongside other horses, and then learned to stride away from them, his working life settles into a pattern.

Two-year-old or experienced chaser, the key to training a racehorse is to combine routine with a specific programme of exercise designed to bring the horse to his peak for a race. But no horse can be at his peak for every race, and the shape of the season – Flat or National Hunt – allows for the biggest events to be prefaced by lesser 'prep' races which normally take less winning.

Thus a top-class staying chaser's programme for the jumping season might be geared towards the twin peaks of the King George VI Chase at Kempton Park on Boxing Day and the Cheltenham Gold Cup at the National Hunt Festival two and a half months later in March. To get the horse to Kempton at peak fitness would probably require one or two earlier outings – say in the Charlie Hall Chase at Wetherby in October or the Tommy Whittle Chase at Haydock in December, or both – and it would not be expected that the horse would be at his peak for those preliminary skirmishes.

A big horse such as a staying chaser takes a very great deal of getting fit, and his annual routine might involve spending the summer at grass before returning to the yard in August. The first few weeks back will be spent simply walking, first for shorter periods then for longer at a time – hours and hours of walking around the roads to develop the leg muscles and start to lose the tummy, the inevitable result of a lazy outdoor summer. Gradually trotting is incorporated into the road work, and then it's back up to the gallops for some light cantering, the amount required gradually increasing as the horse becomes fitter.

Even when the horse is fit the amount and intensity of exercise will be carefully controlled, and he will certainly not gallop every day; this would soon burn out the most enthusiastic competitor. Trainers' routines differ, but in many yards horses will 'work' – that is, have serious gallops – on two days a week. Work is naturally organised around a horse's racing programme, and a horse's main pre-race gallop will probably take place four or five days before the race itself, with a 'pipe-opener' – a short, fast stretch – a couple of days before the race to clear the wind. Few trainers gallop their horses over the full distance of the intended race as that could 'overcook' them by taking them to the limit of their mental or physical capability.

Getting a large, heavy animal like a horse fit in both wind and muscle without over-taxing the legs can be a very tricky assignment, and for this reason increasing numbers of trainers use an equine swimming pool in their training programme. Many horses benefit from swimming, which has the great advantage of working the muscles and cardiovascular system hard but putting no strain on the legs.

Another variation to the routine favoured by many trainers is the occasional racecourse gallop, taking the horse away from the yard and the training ground for a sort of 'dry run'. As well as giving a horse more experience of the racecourse atmosphere – many racecourse gallops take place on race days when the formal programme is over, and offer an extra attraction for racegoers not anxious to beat the traffic – this helps a horse get used to travelling to and from the course, so that it is less likely to waste nervous energy on race day itself.

School days

National Hunt performers, of course, have to be taught to jump as well as gallop – a process which requires great patience from handlers as horses are put through their paces in a 'loose school', jumping over a line of small poles without a rider until their confidence gradually builds and they are ready to attempt a real hurdle or fence.

Chasers and hurdlers are 'schooled' at home over the appropriate obstacles to buff up their jumping skills at the start of the season, but many trainers are reluctant to school during the season unless the horse needs a refresher course after a fall or a particularly bad jumping display. 'The first time I sat on Dessie was a fairly hair-raising experience and left me clear about one thing – never sit on this horse anywhere other than on a racecourse,' wrote Richard Dunwoody of Desert Orchid in his book *Hands and Heels*. He recounts the first time he ever got on Desert Orchid, for a session over David Elsworth's five schooling fences:

He hardly touched the ground, let alone a fence. He was standing off miles and landing just as far out the other side. By the time we landed over the last, Dessie was off. We worked up over a mile. After a good, searching piece of work like that, most horses will pull up. As soon as I stood up in the irons, Dessie, realizing his morning's fun was over, pulled up like a gentleman. Riding him on a racecourse was not going to be a tenth as difficult or hair-raising as riding him at home.

Tom Dreaper once schooled Arkle with his eminent stable companion Flyingbolt. Paddy Woods rode Flyingbolt, and Arkle was partnered by his regular jockey Pat Taaffe, who described how even on the schooling ground the competitive urge took hold:

They took the next four fences, neck and neck, flat out as though their lives depended on the outcome. While Paddy and I just held on to them for dear life and waited for the fires to die down. Well, they cleared them all right, but it was a bit too close for comfort. And Mr Dreaper never allowed them to be schooled together again.

Tom Dreaper was one of the great exponents of the 'old school' of racehorse training. The modern trend is towards an equine version of 'interval training', whereby horses work up a short but stiff uphill gallop, stop at the top then walk back to the foot of the gallop and repeat the process – the number of repetitions depending on the stage of preparation they are at and the level of fitness to which they are being brought.

Once a horse is fit he will remain so for a while with little in the way of serious exercise. What he does once this state is attained depends entirely on the individual. All horses are different. Some can take a great deal of racing over a short period – Chaplins Club, for example, won seven races from nine starts in just nineteen days in the summer of 1988 – while others need a good deal of time to recover from each race. Similarly, some are ready to win first time out, while others need at least a couple of races to get fit. It is part of the trainer's skill to respond to those differences.

Food and drink

Fuel for athletes

A racehorse is usually fed twice a day (early morning and early evening), and its intake of food is carefully adjusted according to its individual needs and tastes and to its racing and training programme. The traditional basic diet is corn – oats (too much of which can get a horse over-excited) – and hay. Many trainers now feed their charges on 'racehorse cubes', manufactured compounds which ensure a balanced diet of high-quality feed. The drawback of cubes is that they can be contaminated by prohibited substances, and the trainer feeding cubes has less control over exactly what he is giving his horses.

Also commonly fed are sugar beet (dried, and then rehydrated by soaking), linseed, molasses, and carrots and apples. A bran mash is a sort of porridge in which the bran is supplemented by oats, treacle or other ingredients to make it more appetising, and perhaps some Epsom salts as a laxative.

Other additives may be less conventional. Arkle's basic feed when in training was a mixture of mash and dry oats mixed up with six eggs and supplemented by two bottles of Guinness, and Mandarin enjoyed a Mackeson: in retirement he had two bottles a day delivered to him from the local pub in Lambourn, courtesy of the late Colonel Bill Whitbread, whose company sponsors the famous handicap chase in which he was three times runner-up.

Junk food and personal fads

Some horses' appetites can try the patience of the most devoted handler ...

- Unsupervised eating can cause problems, and not only ones of nutritional balance: No Bombs, a good hurdler, once filched his lad's Mars Bar, thereby giving himself a dose of the prohibited substance theobromine which the 'work, rest and play' delicacy contains. He ran, won, failed the dope test and forfeited the race.

- Horses, like humans, can be fussy eaters: when the yearling Nijinsky arrived at Ballydoyle from Canada, Vincent O'Brien discovered that he missed the horse nuts he was used to and would not eat oats; so O'Brien had to send across the Atlantic for supplies of the pernickety young horse's familiar food. By the time the nuts arrived in County Tipperary, Nijinsky had taken to eating the oats!

Calming influences and kindred spirits

One of the most intriguing aspects of the lives of horses in training is the company they keep – not just more horses, but a range of other animals: for Thoroughbreds tend to be highly strung, nervous individuals, and in many cases the presence of another creature proves a calming influence.

Often the companion is another equine. The great filly Pebbles – winner of the One Thousand Guineas in 1984 and the Eclipse Stakes, Champion Stakes and Breeders' Cup Turf in 1985 – had a particularly soft spot for a fellow inmate of Clive Brittain's yard, the handicapper Come On The Blues. No impropriety was hinted at – Come On The Blues was a gelding – but the presence of the other horse made Pebbles more placid and amenable, and Come On The Blues got a free weekend in New York when accompanying his friend to Belmont Park for the Turf, causing the *New York Times* to describe him as 'a British gelding she has a crush on'.

Many other well-known horses have found a pony or donkey a good friend. Arkle was accompanied by a donkey named Nellie when recuperating from his career-ending injury, and the friendship of another great Irish chaser, Cottage Rake, for a donkey resulted in disaster. Cottage Rake and the donkey were let out every day in a field, and on one occasion the cattle who spent the night in the field were inadvertently left in when the three-times Gold Cup winner and his chum arrived. The donkey wandered off and soon got among the cattle, and when Cottage Rake could not locate his friend he panicked. Charging round the field in search of the donkey, he slipped at a corner and damaged a tendon. He was never the same horse again.

Words of wisdom from Martin Pipe

In his autobiography *Martin Pipe*, written with Richard Pitman, the trainer reveals a few telling insights into technique:

The way I tell when a horse is ready to run – and I don't run them until they are able to win – is purely by listening to its breathing and monitoring its recovery rate. The fitter a horse is, the quicker he stops blowing and his heart rate returns to normal. I have a particular place by the [all-weather] strip where I stand to listen to their breathing when working and often I close my eyes to sharpen my hearing . . .

To start horses off from grass we walk for a minimum of six weeks, then go straight to cantering. At that stage they may also swim, depending on the amount of fat they are carrying. I'll take as long as is necessary to get a horse fit, although the norm is three months. Once fully fit, horses can take races close together but running fat horses to attain fitness is wrong in my mind. It does more harm than good, putting strain on tendons and muscles when the horse is tiring. People accuse me of being too hard on my horses, but the reverse is true. Mine are never put under stress at home. They are built up gradually, and if they are showing signs of weakness or immaturity, we lay them off.

Like all good horse handlers, I pay attention to a horse's state of mind. Although I do not agree with the change-of-scenery idea, we make a point of giving the animals love and affection in and out of the stable, making sure they feel safe with their surroundings; and we try to make exercise enjoyable, so that they can't wait to get at it in the mornings. By using the pool and the automatic exercisers, schooling youngsters over small jumps or even taking horses up the gallops again, we manage to get most inmates out of their stables twice a day, breaking their confinement up as much as possible.

Many stables have a resident goat for the calming-down role – Foinavon, winner of the grotesque 1967 Grand National, and 1994 Lincoln Handicap heroine Our Rita were both goat-lovers – and that splendid chaser Remittance Man was very attached to sheep: best known of his succession of woolly friends was Nobby, who features in the section of colour photographs later in the book. Allez France, winner of the Prix de l'Arc de Triomphe in 1974 and one of the most popular mares ever to race in France, was also enamoured of a sheep. Sunnyhill, a chaser in Ireland in the 1950s, was more original in his tastes, bestowing his affections on a goose, while 1929 Grand National winner Gregalach went everywhere with a rough-haired terrier.

Chemistry is a strange thing, however, and combinations of horse and would-be friend do not always work out as intended. St Simon, one of the greatest horses to race in the late nineteenth century, was very difficult to manage in his box, so was given a cat as a calming influence. St Simon seized the cat in his mouth, threw it up against the ceiling of his box and killed it.

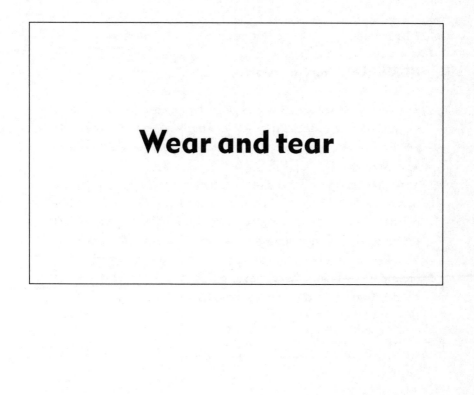

Wear and tear

HORSE SENSE from John Oaksey

The best horse I ever saw was Arkle; in almost every way, he came close to anyone's ideal. But even Pat Taaffe could not always hold him and, having been carted all my life, my ideal horse slows down when you say 'steady'.

Another, more important requirement is a horse who takes care of himself – and his rider. When you asked Tuscan Prince to take off further from a fence than he thought advisable, he did not just gallop straight on and send you into orbit. Tuscy's alternative was to 'fiddle' like a dancer, go up like a lift and lose neither time nor ground. I don't claim he was ever within three stone of Arkle. But he didn't pull, he didn't fall and he gave my family more pleasure than any other horse.

Wear and tear

Ailments and injuries

How many times have you heard that a horse fancied for a big race has 'gone wrong' shortly before the event? Every racing year seems to provide dozens of instances when ante-post backers are left cursing as news comes through that a horse has got a runny nose, or thrown a splint, or coughed, or – having survived intact until the morning of the race – got himself cast in his box.

Like any creature, the horse is subject to all sorts of ailments and injuries, but the nature of the racehorse's calling makes him especially susceptible to stresses and strains on the legs: you only have to think of the impact on the forelegs when landing over a steeplechase fence on firm going to understand why chasers break down so often.

The following are some of the problems that crop up most often in racing.

Back trouble

Horses, like humans, get bad backs: in racehorses, this is often caused by an accident such as falling or slipping up during a race. The jolt or impact can put the spine out of alignment, causing pain and subsequent muscular spasms, which are produced in an effort to protect the damaged area. The acute phase is treated with anti-inflammatory drugs to reduce muscle spasm, allowing the misalignment to be treated by physiotherapists or chiropractors.

A notable example of a horse whose career was blighted by back trouble was Carvill's Hill. His near hindquarter had wasted as a consequence of pelvic damage following a heavy fall in Ireland, and after joining Martin Pipe from Jim Dreaper he was treated by Mary Bromiley, doyenne of equine physiotherapists. Going against the received wisdom that bad backs need rest, she devised remedial exercises to get the muscles working again: these included fitting a four-ounce heavier shoe on Carvill's Hill's near-hind foot than on his off-hind in order to make him use the affected muscle more. The treatment worked so well that in the 1991 Welsh National he produced one of the great chasing performances of the modern era, grinding his opponents into the Chepstow mud to win by twenty lengths.

Breaking blood vessels

It can be a distressing sight when a horse pulls up with blood coming out of its nostrils. The bleeding indicates a haemorrhage in the lungs caused by strenuous exertion, which can be treated by drugs and by a period of rest – anything from a few days to several months. The horse will also be 'scoped', that is, subjected to endoscopic examination of his airways.

While the condition will not necessarily recur every time the horse races, a tendency to break blood vessels is always worrying. A recent example of a well-known horse prone to breaking blood vessels is One Man, who was discovered to be bleeding after being pulled up in the Martell Cup at Aintree in 1997.

'Breaking down': tendon strain

Tendons are the bands of strong tissue that attach muscles to bones. All the muscles in the horse's foreleg are above the knee, and are attached to the bones of the pastern and hoof by the tendons running the length of the lower leg. Obviously, these tendons are subjected to great strain when a horse is galloping, and are placed under particular stress by jumping. Unlike muscles, tendons cannot stretch much, and so are vulnerable to damage under extreme pressure. Uneven going, tired muscles and jolts to the leg all increase the likelihood of tendon strain, which in severe cases causes the tendons to tear and elongate or give way completely – commonly known as 'breaking down'.

A common method of treating tendon strain is 'firing', based on the principle that the scar tissue that will form in response to the application of heat is stronger than the damaged tissue. First a local anaesthetic is applied to the area; then red-hot irons are applied to the damaged tendon. In bar or line firing the iron is drawn across the skin in lines about an inch apart; in pin firing the iron is inserted through the skin into the tissue of the tendon; acid firing involves the application of concentrated sulphuric acid to the skin. Unpleasant as such treatments sound, they are held by many to be very effective, despite opposition in some quarters within the veterinary profession. In 1991 firing was outlawed by the Royal College of Veterinary Surgeons, but there was sufficient professional support for the practice for the ban to lapse, and it is now in common use once more.

A newer method of treating damaged forelegs is the implantation of carbon fibres to strengthen the tendons: the Queen Mother's chaser Special Cargo underwent such treatment and after an absence of two years returned to racing and beat Lettoch and Diamond Edge in the memorable Whitbread Gold Cup of 1984.

Bruised foot

The underside of the foot is quite sensitive in many Thoroughbreds and can fairly easily be damaged. If a horse steps on a large stone it may well bruise the sole and will feel sore and unwilling to put its weight on that foot. A sharp stone or spike – anything that actually punctures the sole – can cause a more serious problem by allowing infection to enter the foot, leading to the build-up of pus. The resulting pressure inside the hoof will cause the horse considerable discomfort and he will be noticeably lame. An infected foot will need to be treated with antibiotics and poulticing – the application of a hot compress to draw the pus out of the foot.

Cast in box

A horse is said to have been 'cast in his box' if he lies down in his stable and then rolls over in such a way that he is trapped by the legs

– often against a wall or under the manger – and cannot get up without assistance. The experience will probably leave him stiff and distressed, especially since it is most likely to occur at night when he may be struggling to free himself for several hours before human assistance arrives. Often a cast horse can only be extricated by being pulled out from the wall or corner with ropes, a process which can add to the trauma.

Colic

The severe abdominal pain known as colic can arise from a variety of causes, including lack of blood supply to the intestines (due to parasitic worm larvae around the blood vessels), impacted foodstuffs or displacements of the bowel. The horse's digestive system is arranged in such a way that it cannot vomit, so any obstruction has to be shifted if the condition is to be eased and serious damage, or even death, prevented. It is usually treated with pain-killing drugs and bowel lubricants, but displacements may call for surgery.

Fractures of the knee

There are ten bones in a horse's knee joint. Repeated stress on the front aspect of these bones can result in 'chip' or 'slab' fractures, which occur most commonly in young horses at the end of a race when the muscles are fatigued, making the knees less stable. The chips can be surgically removed and the larger slabs screwed back into place. The horse must then be rested. Premature resumption of work will only exacerbate the condition.

Heart trouble

Racing can put a great stress on a horse's heart, and detection of a heart murmur or another heart condition casts a serious shadow over a racing career. Recent veterinary research has suggested that as many as 60 per cent of racehorses have some form of heart murmur, although in only a small fraction of cases is this marked enough to impair performance. Large horses tend to be more affected by heart trouble than small. Some well-known horses have overcome heart complaints, including two post-war Cheltenham Gold Cup winners in the shape of Knock Hard and Fort Leney.

Laminitis

In the horse's foot, the pedal bone is connected to the wall of the hoof by a layer of sensitive tissues called the laminae. If these tissues become inflamed the horse will be in great pain, as the horny outside of the hoof cannot expand to accommodate the swelling associated with the inflammation. Though laminitis is most common in overweight ponies, it can occur in racehorses as a result of overfeeding or severe infections; it is treated with pain-killers and appropriate adjustment of diet.

Muscle strains and tears

Like any human athlete, a horse is most likely to tear or strain a muscle when he is tired, and getting to the point where the muscles are exhausted. Muscle strains can be treated with drugs, but – as with so many equine ailments – the key to full recovery is plenty of rest.

Overreaching

When the horse is galloping, the hind feet come very close to the front feet at the end of each stride, and when tired or at full stretch towards the end of the race he may strike into the back of a forefoot with a hind foot, cutting himself just above the heel of the front foot with the front edge of the hind shoe. When this happens the horse is said to have overreached, and the resulting cut is called an overreach.

Soft palate disease

A horse with a soft palate complaint 'swallows his tongue': the horse gurgles and suddenly slows right up, then gets his breath back. What has happened is that the junction between the larynx and the soft palate has become unsealed, causing the passage of air to be obstructed. This usually happens when the horse is under pressure at the climax of a race; once he can swallow and reseal the junction, he recovers. The use of a tongue strap can be an effective counter to this condition: by keeping the tongue in a forward position, it helps to maintain the essential seal between larynx and soft palate.

Sore shins

As with fractures of the knee (see above) or stress fractures (see below), this condition is most common among young racehorses. Fast work or racing on hard ground puts great stress on the legs, and can result in inflammation of the shins.

Spavin

A spavin is an arthritis of the hock. It can often be set off by an awkward movement or accident, but can then become progressively worse without further trauma. Poor conformation of the hock encourages the development of a spavin which, once established, will be a long-term problem.

Splints

Splint bones are small bones between the knee and the fetlock, and a 'splint' is the common name for a bony enlargement of one of these, caused by a kick or by stress on the bones and ligaments. It may look unsightly but does not usually interfere seriously with the horse's long-term prospects.

Split pastern

The pastern is the bone between a horse's fetlock joint and hoof (see the diagram on page 28), and a split pastern is another condition to which young horses are especially susceptible. Repeated concussion causes a hairline fracture vertically through the centre. The injury is usually treated by inserting compression screws across the fracture, but the horse will be out of action for several months.

Stress fractures

Stress fractures in the lower limb, particularly the cannon bone, are common in young horses, whose bones are not mature, and are often caused by repeated concussion of the limbs on a hard surface – hence the danger of running two-year-olds on firm going. (Sore shins in cannon bones – see above – are a form of stress fracture.) Older horses are less prone to stress fractures as their bones are much harder.

Virus

In racing parlance 'the virus' is a catch-all term that covers a variety of respiratory conditions caused by a viral infection of some kind, all of which can spread rapidly in stable yards and on racecourses; often the first sign of the presence of the virus is a lacklustre performance on course. Equine flu is a severe viral respiratory infection: its major symptom is a dry cough – hence the horror of coughing in a racing stable – accompanied by high temperature and a nasal discharge. It usually takes a horse two to three weeks to recover, after which he will need a period of convalescence.

The particular horror of the virus is that once it affects one horse in a stable, it can spread very quickly among the other inmates, and it is not unknown for a stable badly affected to shut up shop while the affliction works its passage. Less severe versions of the malady can simply take the edge off the horses' performance for a while, and when a stable is out of form, a bout of some version of the virus is often the cause.

Whistling and roaring

These are noises caused by paralysis of the vocal cords in the larynx. When the horse breathes in, they flap around in the airway, making noises and obstructing the incoming air. The surgical operation sometimes carried out to remove the vocal cords and ventricles in such cases – to improve the airflow through the larynx – is known as hobdaying, after its originator Sir Frederick Hobday, former Principal of the Royal College of Veterinary Surgeons. That good hurdler Relkeel was hobdayed in 1998, and showed that the operation had left no ill effects when battling to victory in the Bonusprint Bula Hurdle at Cheltenham on his reappearance.

An alternative way of dealing with the problem is to insert a metal tube in the trachea (windpipe) below the larynx to allow the air to bypass the obstruction; this is known as 'tubing', and a horse that has been tubed can be identified by a small hole on the underside of the neck. The 1992 Grand National winner Party Politics, who suffered various wind infirmities over the years, is a prominent example of a tubed horse; he had also undergone a 'tie-back' operation, in which the paralysed muscle in the larynx is replaced with elastic material which keeps the larynx open permanently.

Opposite:
Indian Skimmer, winner of the Prix de Diane in 1987 and the Champion Stakes in 1988, and third in the 1988 Breeders' Cup Turf, with her first foal, a colt by Mr Prospector, in 1991.

Companionship. *Above:* Mare and foal at Juddmonte Farms in Berkshire.
Below: Remittance Man with his chum Nobby the sheep.

At Tattersalls. *Above:* The colt foal by Sadler's Wells sold for 315,000 guineas in December 1998. *Below:* A yearling leaves the ring after the Houghton Sale for a new life as a racehorse, October 1998.

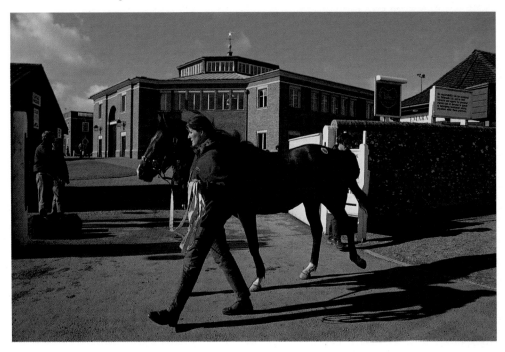

Stallions. *Above:* Nureyev at the Walmac Farm, Lexington, Kentucky.
Below: Cadeaux Genereux stretches his legs at Whitsbury Manor Stud, Hampshire.

Two of jumping's all-time greats. *Above:* Red Rum on the Southport sands.
Below: Desert Orchid and Richard Dunwoody in full flight.

Three champions. *Above:* Shergar (Walter Swinburn) goes to post for the
King George VI and Queen Elizabeth Diamond Stakes at Ascot, 1981.
Below: Cigar and Jerry Bailey after their victory in the 1995 Breeders' Cup
Classic at Belmont Park. *Right:* The grey One Man (Brian Harding) leads the
field in the Queen Mother Champion Chase at Cheltenham in 1998.

Grand old man. Spanish Steps, winner of the 1969 Hennessy Gold
Cup and numerous other big races, in retirement in Oxfordshire.
Thirty-one when this photograph was taken in 1994, he died in 1997.

Death in action

Even a career-ending injury or illness pales into insignificance beside the ultimate horror which racing can – and all too frequently does – provide: the death of a horse in action.

One Man's fatal fall at Aintree in April 1998, in his first race following his greatest moment of glory at Cheltenham the previous month, was the most painful racing experience of the year. But it was by no means a freak occurrence. There are in the region of two hundred equine fatalities on the track every year, and around one in two hundred horses competing in National Hunt races is either killed outright or humanely put down on the course. There are several causes – a broken back, neck or leg after blundering at a jump or falling; a heart attack during the race; a leg snapping while racing along the level – and as soon as the vet has ascertained that there is no hope of healing and connections have agreed, the horse is despatched very quickly. It may seem callous to destroy a horse so readily and with so little thought of repairing the damage and nursing him through a long convalescence, but the brutal fact is that the chances of the animal recovering from a broken limb are very remote indeed – it is not easy for a horse to make a good patient – and putting him down is usually kinder than trying to keep him alive.

One Man was a very high-profile recent casualty, but any jumping fan will recall other horses whose sudden transformation from magnificent athlete to carcass brings that lurch to the stomach – and as often as not a hasty move towards the car park. In addition to One Man and Dawn Run (see page 117), well-known jumpers who have been killed in action over the last two decades include Alverton, Brownes Gazette, Celtic Ryde, Ekbalco, Forgive'N Forget, Golden Cygnet, Killiney, Lanzarote, Noddy's Ryde, Ten Plus, Royal Gait, Pegwell Bay, Cahervillahow, Rushing Wild and Monsieur Le Cure – whose fatal fall in the 1996 Cheltenham Gold Cup was one of ten equine deaths at that year's Festival. Other famous horses, such as Bula and Mighty Mogul, have had to be put down due to serious injuries sustained on the track.

Brown Trix and Seeandem were not in the same league as any of those stars, but their deaths at Becher's Brook in the 1989 Grand National caused such disquiet that the landing side of the fence was modified to reduce the risk.

It is not only in National Hunt racing that deaths in action occur: the Breeders' Cup, world showpiece of Flat racing, has seen fatal accidents in running, notably the deaths of the great American filly Go For Wand in the Distaff at Belmont Park in 1990 and of Richard Hannon's July Cup winner Mr Brooks, ridden by Lester Piggott, in the Sprint at Gulfstream Park in 1992. And in 1998 a British showpiece, the Ascot Gold Cup, was marred by the death of French Ballerina: winner of the Supreme Novices' Hurdle at Cheltenham earlier in the year and a mare of immense promise, she fractured her near hind soon after leaving the stalls at Ascot and was straight away put down. It was the second death in the Ascot Gold Cup in four years: The Little Thief was destroyed after breaking down in the 1995 running.

Accidents can also happen, of course, on the home gallops. Mill Reef's glittering career (see pages 126–7) was brought to a premature end by a mishap at home, but he was saved for a new life at stud. Among horses of recent memory to have suffered a fatal accident at home is the highly popular hurdling mare Mysilv, who fractured a pelvis on the gallops in January 1997 and was put down.

Life after racing

After the hustle and bustle and excitement of the racing life, what then?

For some – but only a few – stud beckons. Most top male performers on the Flat end up as stallions, and the best females as broodmares; but even then, stud duties do not necessarily rule out continuing on the track. Environment Friend, winner of the Eclipse Stakes in 1991, later in his career combined stallion duties with racing; also in 1991, Indian Queen won the Ascot Gold Cup while in foal to Night Shift: the offspring, who won the Gold Cup *in utero*, is Prince Of Spain.

Retirement and re-employment

For the majority of racehorses not destined for a life at stud, career opportunities do not exactly abound. For ex-Flat horses in particular, past their usefulness on the Turf but still young in terms of physical development and experience, the transition from the hothouse atmosphere of a racing yard to the chill wind of the outside world can be a tricky one – however illustrious the pedigree: a card in a newsagent's window in Chipping Norton, Oxfordshire, in December 1998 advertised for sale, next to a card offering a second-hand wardrobe ('divides into two parts – £10') a three-year-old gelding by Bustino 'due to lack of time' . . .

For ex-jumping horses, often older, bigger and more experienced, the range of options may be slightly broader. The 1983 Grand National winner Corbiere had an honourable crack at show jumping, winning several classes: his jumping had always been his great strength, and once he had been trained to change his length of stride and achieve more control and balance than is necessary in the hurly-burly of Aintree, his natural athleticism reasserted itself in the show-jumping ring.

Another Grand National winner, Mr Frisk, turned his hand to eventing – as did 1973 Cheltenham Gold Cup winner The Dikler who, remarkably for such a large and headstrong racehorse, proved a dab hand at the dressage stage. And it is not unknown – though somewhat unusual – for a small ex-racehorse to find employment as a polo pony: Fort Duchesny, winner of one minor race at Windsor in 1985, became one of the best polo ponies in England.

Few Thoroughbreds are temperamentally suited to conversion from racehorse to riding-school hack, though many find good homes with more experienced riders, and it is common for ex-chasers to enjoy a stint following hounds in their twilight years. (Hunting is also a highly effective pick-me-up frequently used for horses in training who have become jaded or bored.) Closely related to hunting is point-to-point racing, and former racehorses are a common sight in the point-to-point field (which can also serve as a nursery for aspiring chasers).

Grand Canyon, a marvellous chaser in the mid-Seventies and dual winner of the Colonial Cup in South Carolina, joined the Household Cavalry, but was not an unqualified success: habits acquired as a racehorse were not easily shrugged off, and Grand Canyon took exception to being required to perform very specific turns or trot in a suitably stately manner. Eventually he too was retired to a more congenial life in the hunting field.

Among the plum retirement jobs for Thoroughbreds is that of trainer's hack. Devon Loch, whose sensational slide on the run-in denied the Queen Mother victory in the 1956 Grand National, became hack to Noel Murless, Tingle Creek to Tom Jones, Comedy Of Errors to Mercy Rimell, and What A Buck to David Nicholson, who explains: 'The horse is living in an environment to which he is accustomed and is kept fit and busy.' Special Cargo, the Queen Mother's Whitbread Gold Cup winner, was tried out as Julie Cecil's hack but soon disgraced himself by setting off up the gallops with the two-year-olds – not the idea at all – and was promptly despatched to a more placid retirement home at Sandringham.

Other old hands, such as Path Of Peace and Shiny Copper, have played their part in educating the next generation of jockeys at the British Racing School at Newmarket or its sister school at Doncaster.

Red Rum, a celebrity on the racetrack, became equally feted off it, his services much in demand for personal appearances opening supermarkets and betting shops, and a similar devotion to public service has kept Desert Orchid busy.

Some ex-racehorses – including familiar National Hunt names Gainsay and South Parade – have found a new niche as police horses. Among these, Casamayor, fourth in the 1979 Cheltenham Gold Cup, carried the Commissioner of Police at the Trooping the Colour and got stuck in during the Wapping riots in 1986.

Rescue and rehabilitation

And yet, for all the pleasure afforded by the sight of an old racehorse picking at grass in a field or beautifully turned out for Trooping the Colour, some have a less pleasant time of it once their racing careers are over. Even well-known horses suffer from neglect, and in recent years a few high-profile cases have stimulated an increase in concern about the fate of ex-racehorses. Daarkom, winner of the Ebor Handicap in 1987, went through various hands and fell on hard times before his plight was discovered and he was revived with a suitable dose of tender loving care. Walnut Wonder, a good hurdler and chaser, won fourteen races and over £90,000 in prize money, but still found himself on equine Skid Row: arthritic, skinny and with failing sight, he was found in a small paddock without food or shelter, and his plight was reported to the RSPCA. He was taken in by the Glenda Spooner Trust (now part of the International League for the Protection of Horses), where his condition – and spirits – revived.

Every racehorse deserves a better fate than neglect, but it is still particularly poignant to learn of a Grand National winner who hit the lows. Hallo Dandy, who beat Greasepaint and Corbiere at Liverpool in 1984, was retired after running unplaced in the 1986 National and leased by his owners for hunting. He spent the next few years following hounds, but by 1994 this magnificent chaser was showing serious physical deterioration, and it was even contemplated that he should be put down. Enter a rescuer in the shape of Carrie Humble, founder of the Thoroughbred Rehabilitation Centre, then based in Kendal, a charity dedicated to re-educating unwanted racehorses and finding them new owners in different walks of life. Ms Humble reported that Hallo Dandy 'had given up the ghost' – but again an infusion of TLC brought about a striking restoration, and the old campaigner is now the flagship of the Thoroughbred Rehabilitation Centre in their new quarters near Preston, Lancashire.

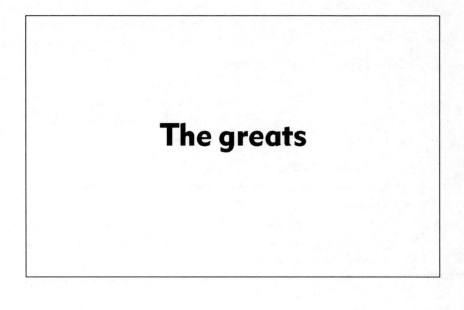

The greats

HORSE SENSE from Jim McGrath

As someone whose job at the races entails considerable time studying horses paddock-side, I look for a combination of qualities. Three in particular are easy to spot:

- presence: basically, a look of alertness and interest;
- paces: an easy, rhythmic walker whose hind leg almost covers the stride made by its foreleg;
- condition: look at the skin – even a clipped-out jumper on a rainy day in winter will advertise his well-being through the sheen on his skin.

Three things I dislike:

- wall-eyed horses;
- horses who muck around in the paddock;
- mulishness, especially fillies who rear up, won't walk on, or even plant themselves.

Big horses tend to take the eye more than small ones. King Of Kings made his racecourse debut as a two-year-old at The Curragh on Irish Derby day 1997, and he just knocked you out as soon as he entered the paddock: big and imposing, he looked every inch a racehorse. I felt the same about Zafonic when I first saw him as a two-year-old at Longchamp, and in both cases their racecourse performances matched their looks.

Looks aren't everything, though, and the picture is not complete until you've seen a horse move, which is why it's essential to allow yourself time to watch the runners going to post.

If a horse looks the part and has an action to match, generally you're in business.

The greats

Fantasy racing. If Arkle, Red Rum and Desert Orchid met at level weights in a three mile five furlong steeplechase at Sandown Park, which of the Railway Fences would Dessie be crossing as Arkle passed the winning post . . . ?

Discussion of the relative merits of different racehorses throughout history is one of the great diversions of racing. Your own favourite may be a lowly selling plater who rescued your punting fortunes when the last pound was down, or simply a character who caught your imagination, but there is some consensus about the handful of true all-time greats. Move one rung down, however, from the undoubted Olympians to the possibly-greats, the there-or-thereabouts-greats, and the picture rapidly blurs: perhaps no two individuals' lists of the top twenty would be identical.

Mark Twain famously observed that it is the difference of opinion that makes horse racing, and it is in that spirit that twenty great racehorses are chronicled on the following pages.

(The description of each horse in the heading – colt, gelding, etc. – is that which applied as that horse was running his or her final race.)

Arkle

bay gelding by Archive out of Bright Cherry
1957–1970 (raced 1961–1966)
ran 35 races; won 27

Arkle was a freak. The bare facts of his career – winner of twenty-two of his twenty-six steeplechases, including the Cheltenham Gold Cup in 1964, 1965 and 1966, the Hennessy Gold Cup in 1964 and 1965, the Whitbread Gold Cup and King George VI Chase in 1965, the Irish National in 1964 – tell only part of the story. For Arkle was so transcendentally good that the rules of handicapping in Ireland had to be changed to allow for his superiority, with one set of weights framed to include 'Himself' (as he was widely known in his home country), another to be applied when he wasn't running.

Bred in modest circumstances in County Dublin, Arkle was bought by Anne, Duchess of Westminster at public auction as a three-year-old for 1,150 guineas and went into training with Tom Dreaper. In his first two outings (both amateur riders' races on the Flat) he was beaten; then, in a novice hurdle at Navan in January 1962, he scored at 20–1, prompting Dreaper to remark to his wife Betty as they came down from the stands, in one of racing's great understatements: 'Do you know, I think we've got something there!'

Some inkling of exactly what they had soon began to emerge. After three more wins over hurdles Arkle was sent across to Cheltenham for his debut over fences: he won that, and everything else he took part in for the remainder of the 1962–3 season. This was clearly an exceptional young horse; but so too was his exact contemporary Mill House – Irish-bred like Arkle, but trained in Lambourn by Fulke Walwyn – who at just six years of age had scored a precocious victory in the 1963 Cheltenham Gold Cup.

The rivalry between these two great horses made the mid-1960s a golden age of British steeplechasing. Their first meeting, in the 1963 Hennessy Gold Cup at Newbury, saw Arkle lose his chance when slipping after the final ditch; Mill House powered home to an easy victory. Thus the scene was set for the famous Cheltenham Gold Cup in March 1964, perhaps the most keenly anticipated horse race since the Second World War. Mill House was favourite at 13–8 on, with Arkle at 7–4, while the only other runners King's Nephew and Pas Seul were priced at 20–1 and 50–1 respectively. By the second circuit the big two had the race to themselves; then, on the run to the last, Arkle – ridden as in all his chases by Pat Taaffe – cruised into the lead and charged up the hill to win by five lengths.

Mark Hely-Hutchinson, who rode as an amateur for Tom Dreaper's stable, has the distinction of being the only jockey to have ridden Arkle in a race and never won on him. Pat Taaffe won twenty-four times on the horse, Liam McLoughlin once, Paddy Woods once and T. P. Burns once (Arkle's sole victory on the Flat).

When the pair met again in the following autumn's Hennessy Gold Cup, Arkle had it all his own way, sweeping imperiously to victory while Mill House crumpled to finish only fourth. A week later the champion delivered one of his greatest performances in the Massey-Ferguson Gold Cup at Cheltenham (now the Tripleprint Gold Cup), failing only narrowly, under the crushing burden of twelve stone ten pounds, to pin back two very high-class and lightly weighted horses, Flying Wild and Buona Notte. Undaunted, he went on through that season to win the Leopardstown Chase in Ireland, a second Cheltenham Gold Cup from Mill House, and the Whitbread under twelve stone seven pounds.

Perhaps his greatest race of all came in November 1965, in the Gallaher Gold Cup at Sandown Park. This was the fifth time he and Mill House had raced against each other, and this time Arkle displayed stunning acceleration on the final turn to surge past his rival (who was eventually passed by Rondetto to finish third), to whom he was conceding sixteen pounds, and go on to win in a time which beat the course record by seventeen seconds!

Arkle looked invincible. He won the Hennessy again, the King George (the running in which the great two-mile chaser Dunkirk was killed), the Leopardstown Chase and a third Gold Cup. He had amassed a huge popular following, drew vast crowds every time he raced, was deluged with fan mail (some addressed simply to 'Arkle, Ireland') and even had a song recorded about him by Dominic Behan. And he was still only nine years old.

But, though no one knew it as the 1966–7 season opened, there were to be only three more races. First time out, in the Hennessy, he was beaten half a length by Stalbridge Colonist, to whom he was conceding thirty-five pounds. Victory in the SGB Chase at Ascot re-established the normal state of affairs, and the King George was widely seen as a formality: his starting price at Kempton was 9–2 on. Here disaster struck. Leading over the last, Arkle was passed on the run-in by Dormant, a horse whom in the normal course of events he could have picked up and carried. The reason for this sensational outcome was not far to seek: Arkle was badly lame and could scarcely hobble into the unsaddling enclosure. He had cracked the pedal bone in his off-fore hoof, and would never race again.

Since Timeform first started rating National Hunt horses in the 1960s, the five highest-rated performers have been:

Arkle 212
Flyingbolt 210
Mill House 191
Desert Orchid 187
Dunkirk 186

Arkle retired to the Duchess of Westminster's Irish home, Bryanstown, where he remained until, stiffness in the joints causing him increasing discomfort, on 31 May 1970 he was put down. He was thirteen.

His skeleton can be seen in the Irish Horse Museum just outside Kildare.

Brigadier Gerard

1968–1989 (raced 1970–1972)
bay colt by Queen's Hussar out of La Paiva
ran 18 races; won 17

Arguably the finest miler of the post-war period in Europe, Brigadier Gerard was never beaten at that distance and did not taste defeat at all until his sixteenth outing.

Brigadier Gerard was home-bred by his owners John and Jean Hislop and sent to trainer Dick Hern at West Ilsley. Four wins from four races as a two-year-old in 1970 (the last of these the Middle Park Stakes at Newmarket) made the colt an outstanding prospect for the 1971 Two Thousand Guineas, but in that race he was opposed by two horses officially rated his superior as juveniles, Mill Reef and My Swallow, and The Brigadier (who did not have a preliminary outing) started third favourite at 11–2. Ridden as in all his races by Joe Mercer, Brigadier Gerard powered down the stands side to win by three lengths from Mill Reef. He ran five more times in 1971, winning the St James's Palace Stakes at Royal Ascot, Sussex Stakes at Goodwood, Goodwood Mile, Queen Elizabeth II Stakes at Ascot and Champion Stakes at Newmarket.

Brigadier Gerard remained in training as a four-year-old and straight away resumed the winning habit, mopping up the Lockinge Stakes at Newbury, Westbury Stakes at Sandown Park (nowadays named the Brigadier Gerard Stakes in his honour), Prince of Wales Stakes at Royal Ascot and Eclipse Stakes. The last three of those races were over a mile and a quarter, widely thought to be the limit of the horse's stamina, but the Hislops were adventurous campaigners, and Brigadier Gerard was stepped up to one and a half miles for the 1972 King George VI and Queen Elizabeth Stakes at Ascot. Here his connections' boldness was rewarded with a hard-fought victory over Parnell and Riverman to give him fifteen wins out of fifteen races.

Mill Reef had also remained in training, and another clash between these two greats in the inaugural Benson and Hedges Gold Cup over a mile and a quarter at York was eagerly awaited. Then an injury to Mill Reef during his preparation seemed to leave the race at The Brigadier's mercy. He started at 3–1 on, but Roberto, ridden by Panamanian jockey Braulio Baeza and starting at 12–1 (an insulting price for the current Derby winner) scorched out of the gate and led all the way to win by three lengths: 'He must have been stung by a bee,' commented Jean Hislop.

Brigadier Gerard, whose sire was Queen's Hussar, was named after an Arthur Conan Doyle character: an officer in the Hussars de Conflan in Napoleon's army.

Brigadier Gerard may have been beaten at last but he remained a hugely popular performer, and racegoers poured along to Ascot to see him right his crown with a six-length victory over Sparkler in the Queen Elizabeth II Stakes – then flocked to Newmarket for the Champion Stakes, raising the roof when he outgalloped Riverman in a glorious finale to a glorious racing career.

His time at stud was less distinguished, with only one English Classic winner to his name: Light Cavalry (1980 St Leger). He died in 1989 at the age of twenty.

Brown Jack

brown gelding by Jackdaw out of Querquidella
1924–1948 (raced 1927–1934)
ran 65 races; won 25

One of the greatest stayers of the century and one of the most popular horses ever to run in Britain, Brown Jack was bred in Ireland, and after two unsuccessful outings as a three-year-old in that country (he did not run at two) was sold to Sir Harold Wernher for £750, with an extra £50 to be paid if the horse ever won a race. In the event, he won twenty-five.

Brown Jack made his English debut in September 1927 over hurdles at Bournemouth, finishing third. He won his next race, over timber at Wolverhampton, and developed into such a fine hurdler that by the end of the 1927–8 season he had won seven races, notably the second ever running of the Champion Hurdle at Cheltenham, for which the four-year-old Brown Jack started at 4–1 and earned Sir Harold £680.

A small bronze of Brown Jack is displayed annually at Ascot during the running of the Brown Jack Stakes, a two-mile handicap commemorating one of the course's greatest heroes.

That Champion Hurdle victory caught the eye of the great jockey Steve Donoghue, who suggested to Brown Jack's then trainer Aubrey Hastings that the horse should run on the Flat. Rarely in racing has better advice been given. By the end of his illustrious career Brown Jack had won eighteen races on the level from fifty-five outings, including the Ascot Stakes (1928), Goodwood Cup (1929), Doncaster Cup (1930),

Chester Cup (1931, carrying nine stone six pounds) and Ebor Handicap (1931, under nine stone five pounds).

But the Queen Alexandra Stakes at Royal Ascot, at two and three-quarter miles the longest distance in the Flat calendar, was the race which Brown Jack really made his own. He first won this marathon in 1929, three days after finishing runner-up in the Ascot Stakes at the same meeting, and proceeded to repeat the achievement five times in a row. The scenes following his sixth victory at the age of ten in 1934 have been famously described by Steve Donoghue, who rode him in most of his races on the Flat, including all six victories in the Queen Alexandra: 'Never will I forget the roar of that crowd as long as I live. Ascot or no Ascot, they went mad. I have never seen so many hats flung in the air, and I have never heard such shrieks of joy in my life.' Ivor Anthony, who following the death of Aubrey Hastings in 1929 had trained Brown Jack for most of his career, had not been able to watch the race, and had sat under a tree in the paddock until the noise from the crowd told him that Brown Jack had duly won.

Brown Jack, a horse of great character who liked nothing better than leaning against his manger and having a kip, died at his owner's home in 1948.

Cigar

bay horse by Palace Music out of Solar Slew
1990– (raced 1993–1996)
ran 33 races; won 19

One of the greatest American racehorses of the modern era, Cigar raked in prize money of US$9,999,813 in a career which saw him equal the US record of sixteen consecutive victories, set by Citation in 1948, and win two of the most valuable races in the world – the Breeders' Cup Classic and the Dubai World Cup.

A son of 1984 Champion Stakes winner Palace Music, Cigar was bred by his owner Allen Paulson and trained for most of his career by Bill Mott. His early races were mostly on turf courses and gave no hint that he was anything out of the ordinary – he won just one race on grass – but when towards the end of his four-year-old year he started concentrating on races on dirt, his fortunes started to soar: his last two races that season produced two victories, including a seven-length triumph in the Grade One NYRA Handicap.

As a five-year-old he won ten successive races, culminating in the Breeders' Cup Classic at Belmont Park from L'Carriere. By this time he had become a national hero; but the international stage beckoned, and after winning his first race of 1996 at Gulfstream Park Cigar was sent to the Middle East for the inaugural running of the Dubai World Cup – which he won in gutsy style after a memorable duel up the straight with compatriot Soul Of The Matter.

That race, Cigar's only outing outside North America, marked his fourteenth consecutive victory, and Citation's record of sixteen in a row, set half a century earlier, was in sight. Win number fifteen duly came in the Massachusetts Handicap at Suffolk Downs; then, in July 1996, Cigar went to Arlington Park, Chicago, for the Arlington Citation

Challenge, a race specially framed for his record attempt. He won by three and a half lengths. The record was matched; but sadly he was not able to better it, thwarted by Dare And Go in the Pacific Classic at Del Mar in his next race. Nevertheless, he resumed the winning habit in the Woodward Stakes at Belmont, before being narrowly beaten by Skip Away in the Jockey Club Gold Cup at the same track and suffering another defeat in what turned out to be his final race, the Breeders' Cup Classic at Woodbine, Toronto, where he was beaten a nose and a head by Alphabet Soup and Louis Quatorze. It was a downbeat ending to a phenomenal career, with twelve of his nineteen victories coming in Grade One events.

Cigar's career earnings of $9,999,813 were a world record at the end of 1998 – though with some bending of exchange rates a case can be made that the ¥1,026,916,000 earned by the Japanese horse Narita Brian (who died in 1998) was in fact greater.

Cigar proved infertile after being retired to the Ashford Stud in Kentucky, but failure as a stallion could in no way diminish the place he held in the hearts of Americans and the racing community worldwide. A tough, battling campaigner who really dug deep in his races, his appeal was summed up by one journalist seeking to explain the defeats once the horse was past his best: Cigar, he said, 'was only human'.

Dancing Brave

bay colt by Lyphard out of Navajo Princess
1983– (raced 1985–1986)
ran 10 races; won 8

Dancing Brave's hammering past the best of Europe's middle-distance horses in the 1986 Prix de l'Arc de Triomphe remains one of the benchmark performances of recent times, and Dancing Brave himself one of the star turns of post-war racing in Europe.

Bred in the United States and bought by his owner Khalid Abdullah for 200,000 guineas as a yearling, Dancing Brave was trained in Sussex by Guy Harwood, who made sure that the horse was not overexposed as a two-year-old: he contested just two small races, both of which he won.

In 1986 Dancing Brave warmed up for the Two Thousand Guineas with a smooth victory in the Craven Stakes at Newmarket, then returned to the same course for the Classic itself and charged home three lengths clear of Green Desert.

When Dancing Brave ran in the Select Stakes at Goodwood in September 1986 as his warm-up race before the Arc, he was such a stone-cold certainty that no starting price was returned.

Next stop Epsom for the Derby – and a race brimming with controversy. Despite worries about his stamina over the trip of a mile and a half, Dancing Brave was sent off 2–1 favourite, with Dante Stakes winner Shahrastani second market choice at 11–2. Those doubts about the colt's staying power prompted Greville Starkey to keep the favourite well back, and Dancing Brave was still third last at Tattenham Corner.

Once the field hit the home straight Starkey pulled the Guineas winner to the outside and Dancing Brave started to devour the ground. But Shahrastani was by now in full flight and not stopping, and as the final furlongs slipped away it became horribly obvious to Dancing Brave's legion of supporters that his jockey had been cutting it very fine – too fine, as Shahrastani kept up his gallop all the way to the finish, and despite Dancing Brave's surge was still half a length to the good at the line. Arguments raged about whether Dancing Brave should have won, but the cold fact of the entry in the form book was that the colt had suffered his first defeat.

A four-length victory over Triptych in the Eclipse Stakes eased the pain a little, and then came the re-match with Shahrastani in the King George VI and Queen Elizabeth Diamond Stakes at Ascot. It was no contest: Dancing Brave – now ridden by Pat Eddery – set the record straight by sweeping past not only Shahrastani but also Shardari and Triptych, leaving the Derby winner back in fourth.

Then, after a facile victory in his prep race at Goodwood, came the Arc. Red-hot opposition included Bering, winner of the Prix du Jockey-Club; German challenger Acatenango, who had won his last twelve races; the redoubtable mare Triptych; Shardari, who since the King George had won the International at York; and Shahrastani again. By any standards this was one of the best renewals of Europe's biggest race for many a year. Cool as ever despite the quality of the opposition, Pat Eddery on Dancing Brave waited until all the other jockeys had made their moves, then produced Dancing Brave for a sweeping run up the outside to win from Bering. It was a devastating performance.

Champion of Europe, then; but there were other worlds to conquer, and Dancing Brave – who had been syndicated for stud purposes even before the Eclipse Stakes at a valuation of £14 million – travelled to California in an attempt to end his career in a blaze of glory in the Breeders' Cup Turf at Santa Anita. He started at 2–1 on but could finish only fourth behind Manila: yet another case of a great horse being taken to the well once too often.

Dancing Brave did not race again. He spent five years at stud in Britain – his fertility affected by his contracting Marie's Disease – before being sold to Japan, where he was already established as a stallion when in 1993 his son Commander In Chief, product of his third crop in Britain, won the Derby.

Dawn Run

bay mare by Deep Run out of Twilight Slave
1978–1986 (raced 1982–1986)
ran 35 races; won 21

The only horse ever to have won both the Champion Hurdle and the Cheltenham Gold Cup, Dawn Run was foaled on a farm in County Cork and sold at auction as a three-year-old for 5,800 guineas to Mrs Charmian Hill, then sixty-two years old and famed throughout Ireland as 'The Galloping Granny': in 1973 Mrs Hill had become the first woman in Ireland to ride against men under Rules. Dawn Run was put into training with Paddy Mullins and made her debut in a bumper at Clonmel in May 1982, ridden by her indefatigable owner. They were beaten, but two races later won at Tralee – Mrs Hill's last ride.

Dawn Run soon developed into a very good hurdler indeed, good enough to be a serious contender for the Sun Alliance Novices' Hurdle at the 1983 Cheltenham Festival. Second there to Sabin Du Loir, she then went to Aintree to win a valuable handicap hurdle under top weight and the following day finished runner-up to Gaye Brief, the current Champion Hurdler, in the Sun Templegate Hurdle. Such a schedule was already proclaiming her a mare of extraordinary toughness.

Early the following season her trainer's son Tony Mullins, who had ridden the mare in most of her races, was replaced by Jonjo O'Neill, and the partnership reversed placings with Gaye Brief in the Christmas Hurdle at Kempton Park in December 1983 before landing the Irish Champion Hurdle. With Gaye Brief sidelined by injury Dawn Run started odds-on favourite for the 1984 Champion Hurdle, and won narrowly from Cima. Later that season she won the Grande Course de

Haies at Auteuil in Paris to complete a hat-trick of English, Irish and French hurdling crowns.

She was switched to steeplechasing for the 1984–5 season but, hampered by injury, managed only one run that term, at Navan in November 1984: nevertheless, she made it a winning one. It was over a year before she was seen out again, and though sights were firmly set on the Cheltenham Gold Cup, her preparation was far from ideal. In her final prep race at Cheltenham she unseated Tony Mullins at the ditch at the top of the hill, and again Jonjo O'Neill was called up for the big occasion.

Dawn Run is one of three great Cheltenham horses commemorated by statues at the course. The others are Golden Miller and Arkle.

And what an occasion the 1986 Gold Cup turned out to be! After being headed between the last two fences, Dawn Run staged a remarkable rally up the run-in to collar Wayward Lad close home and trigger such scenes of delirious excitement that over a decade later there are still Cheltenham racegoers looking for their hats. A unique feat had been achieved by a mare whose connections and whose own dogged character epitomised the gigantic Irish contribution to jump racing, and Cheltenham's euphoria was unbounded.

After the hysteria came anti-climax, followed by tragedy. Dawn Run fell at the first fence in the Whitbread Gold Label Cup at Liverpool, then won a match over two miles at Punchestown against Buck House, winner of the Queen Mother Champion Chase. In early June 1986 she was second in the Prix la Barka at Auteuil, and at the end of that month attempted a repeat victory in the Grand Course de Haies. This time she was ridden by French jockey Michel Chirol, and the mare was a close-up third when at the fifth last hurdle she fell heavily, broke her neck and died instantly. She was eight years old.

Desert Orchid

grey gelding by Grey Mirage out of Flower Child
1979– (raced 1983–1991)
ran 72 races; won 34

Not many racehorses find their way into the Chancellor of the Exchequer's Budget speech, but it is a mark of how intense the public adulation of 'Dessie' became that Norman Lamont sought to ingratiate himself with the electorate by mentioning the great grey in the House of Commons in 1991. A poll had shown that while 84 per cent of people had heard of Dessie only 77 per cent had heard of Lamont, and the Chancellor saw his chance: 'Desert Orchid and I have a lot in common. We are both greys, vast sums of money are riding on our performance, the opposition hopes we will fall at the first fence, and we are both carrying too much weight.' Ho ho, very droll . . .

Desert Orchid ran once on the Flat. Ridden by Brian Rouse, he finished tenth of eleven runners behind Longboat in the Sagaro Stakes at Ascot in May 1985.

It is not difficult to understand why Desert Orchid so touched a public nerve. His bold, front-running style of racing, his flamboyant, attacking attitude towards jumping fences, and his sheer physical appearance – a big, headstrong grey oozing power and enthusiasm – made up a heady cocktail. In a racing career which spanned nearly nine years he rarely let down his fans or his connections: owner Richard Burridge, trainer David Elsworth and regular jockeys Colin Brown,

Simon Sherwood (who won on nine out of his ten rides on the horse) and latterly Richard Dunwoody.

But the glory days were a far cry from his racecourse debut, in a novices' hurdle at Kempton Park in January 1983: he fell at the final obstacle, and for a while, as he failed to rise from the ground, it seemed that his first race would be his last. But he was only winded, and after ten minutes prostrate heaved himself up to continue his way into the hearts of the racing public. That first season he failed to win from four runs, but in the 1983–4 term developed into a very fine hurdler, winning six of his seven starts before running unplaced behind Dawn Run in the Champion Hurdle. The following year was less productive, but the switch from hurdling to chasing in winter 1985 proved an immediate success, with victories in several top novice events.

By Boxing Day 1986 Desert Orchid was already one of the most popular chasers in training, but he was thought to be a two-mile specialist rather than a horse who would excel at the top-level staying events, and he was allowed to start at 16–1 for the three-mile King George VI Chase at Kempton Park against the likes of Wayward Lad, Forgive'N Forget and Combs Ditch. His performance belied the odds, and after a sensational display of front running had left those distinguished rivals toiling in his wake as he won by fifteen lengths, Dessie was firmly in the top flight.

In the 1987 King George he finished second to Nupsala, then later that season won the Chivas Regal Cup at Aintree and raised the roof at Sandown Park when beating Kildimo in the 1988 Whitbread Gold Cup.

A second King George victory in 1988 put him right up there with the best post-war chasers, but to seal his place in the pantheon he needed to win the Cheltenham Gold Cup, and therein lay a problem. Cheltenham had never been one of Desert Orchid's favourite places, and the fact that he had not won there was widely attributed to his dislike of left-handed tracks, the single win at Aintree being his only anti-clockwise victory to date. On Gold Cup day 1989 his chances seemed further diminished by a deluge of rain and snow that turned the track into a quagmire – heavy conditions which the horse hated. But he overcame all adversities, battling up the hill to get the better of Yahoo just before the post in one of the most emotional races of the modern era.

Now a national institution – complete with his own fan club – Desert Orchid continued his winning ways. In the 1989–90 season he won a third King George VI Chase and put up a brilliant weight-carrying performance when humping twelve stone three pounds to victory in the Racing Post Chase at Kempton. He finished third behind Norton's Coin and Toby Tobias in the Gold Cup, but then went on to win the Irish Grand National at Fairyhouse – his only victory outside Britain – under twelve stone.

The following season he won a record fourth King George amid scenes of huge enthusiasm at Kempton, lugged twelve stone to victory in the Agfa Diamond Chase at Sandown – in what turned out to be his last win – and again finished third in the Gold Cup, this time behind Garrison Savannah and The Fellow. By the time of his sixth consecutive King George on Boxing Day 1991 Dessie was a few days short of his thirteenth birthday, and the power was beginning to fade. But he still managed to hog the limelight – falling at the third last fence when out of contention, then galloping Dunwoody-less past the stands to a wildly appreciative farewell from his adoring fans.

Desert Orchid ran once in blinkers – in the Welsh Champion Hurdle at Chepstow in April 1985. He was pulled up.

In retirement his public appearances became a regular feature of big racing occasions, and his continuing popularity was nowhere more evident than on his annual outing to head the parade before the King George VI Chase: on Boxing Day 1998, a few days short of his twentieth birthday, he yet again drew rapturous applause from the Kempton crowd. But it is the sight of Desert Orchid in action – powering towards a fence, bouncing into the air yards before it and landing straight back into that relentless gallop – which will long remain in racing's collective memory.

Eclipse

chestnut horse by Marske out of Spiletta
1764–1789 (raced 1769–1770)
ran 18 races; won 18

Eclipse, foaled in 1764 and named after the great eclipse of the sun in the year of his birth, was bred by the Duke of Cumberland, and on the Duke's death in 1765 was bought by William Wildman, a Smithfield meat salesman, for 75 guineas. His new owner was in no hurry to race Eclipse, and the horse was given ample time to mature, going into serious training only at the age of five. In April 1769 Wildman held a trial on Banstead Downs, near Epsom; it was to be kept secret, but none the less – according to a contemporary report – some touts did their best to get a sneak preview of this new prospect. Turning up too late to see the action, instead 'they found an old woman who gave them all the information they wanted. On inquiring whether she had seen a race, she replied she could not tell whether it was a race or not, but she had just seen a horse with a white leg running away at a monstrous rate, and another horse a great way behind, trying to run after him; but she was sure he never would catch the white-legged horse if he ran to the world's end.'

The skeleton of Eclipse is one of the prize exhibits at the National Horseracing Museum in Newmarket.

A month later Eclipse – the 'horse with a white leg' – had his first outing in public, at Epsom in a race of four-mile heats. Starting favourite at 4–1 on following rumours of the trial, he won the first heat with ease, prompting an Irish gambler called Dennis O'Kelly to bet that he could predict the placings of the runners in the next heat in their correct finishing order. When his challenge was taken up he uttered the phrase which was to become part of racing language: 'Eclipse first, the rest nowhere.' His prediction – that all the other runners would be 'distanced' by Eclipse (that is, finish over 240 yards behind him) – was proved triumphantly correct, and O'Kelly went on to purchase a half share in the horse for 650 guineas; later he bought the other half too, by which time the price had risen to 1,100 guineas: no mean sum for the eighteenth century.

In eighteen races Eclipse was never whipped or spurred; yet he was never headed, let alone beaten. Retiring to stud in 1771, he sired three of the first five Derby winners.

How Eclipse bred Swain . . .

> ECLIPSE
> Pot-8-os
> Waxy
> Whalebone
> Sir Hercules
> Birdcatcher
> The Baron
> Stockwell
> Doncaster
> Bend Or
> Bona Vista
> Cyllene
> Polymelus
> Phalaris
> Pharos
> Nearco
> Nasrullah
> Red God
> Blushing Groom
> Nashwan
> SWAIN

Golden Miller

bay gelding by Goldcourt out of Miller's Pride
1927–1957 (raced 1930–1939)
ran 55 races; won 29

Winner of the Cheltenham Gold Cup five times and the only horse ever to win the Gold Cup and Grand National in the same year, Golden Miller remains a giant of National Hunt racing sixty years after his racing career came to an end.

Golden Miller was foaled near Dublin in 1927, sold as a yearling at public auction for 120 guineas, then sold on as an unbroken three-year-old to trainer Basil Briscoe for 500 guineas. He ran his first race at three in a two-mile hurdle at Southwell in September 1930, and at Leicester on his third outing scored his first win, thereby confounding some in the Briscoe yard who had thought the young horse slow, clumsy and unwilling.

Golden Miller ran three times on the Flat – at Warwick and Newmarket in April 1931, and at Liverpool in March 1932.

The Hon. Dorothy Paget, then a newcomer to racehorse ownership, allegedly spent £12,000 to acquire Golden Miller and the hurdler Insurance before the 1931–2 season, and her investment was rewarded the following March when on the same afternoon Golden Miller won his first Cheltenham Gold Cup – at the tender age of five – and Insurance the first of his two Champion Hurdles.

Golden Miller ran up a sequence of five straight wins the following year, including a second Gold Cup from Thomond II, before going to Liverpool for the 1933 Grand National, the first of his five runs in the race. Starting 9–1 favourite, he blundered badly at second Becher's and finally unshipped jockey Ted Leader at the Canal Turn. By the time he returned for another attempt in 1934 he had won a third Gold Cup, beating Avenger and the previous year's National winner Kellsboro' Jack: carrying twelve stone two pounds round Aintree and starting 8–1 second favourite, he won by five lengths.

Golden Miller proceeded to run up another five-timer the next season, culminating in the famous battle with Thomond in the Gold Cup. From the third last, down the hill and all the way up the straight, Thomond and Golden Miller were at it hammer and tongs, until close home the Miller edged ahead and won by three-quarters of a length. Then it was back to Liverpool – and disaster. At 2–1 the shortest-priced favourite in Grand National history, Golden Miller was already trailing by the eleventh fence, where he attempted to refuse and then, having been persuaded to cross the jump, unshipped Gerry Wilson. The following day he came out again for the Champion Chase – and this time unseated Wilson at the first fence. Owner–trainer relations, strained at the best of times, snapped, and Briscoe demanded the removal of the Paget horses from his yard. So it was under the care of Owen Anthony that Golden Miller won his fifth consecutive Cheltenham Gold Cup in 1936, beating Royal Mail (who would win the 1937 National) and Kellsboro' Jack. But again the National proved a fiasco, with Golden Miller brought down at the first fence, then remounted before refusing at the eleventh – his bogey fence from the previous year.

The 1937 Gold Cup was lost to the weather, but Golden Miller was yet again in the line-up at Liverpool for the Grand National. He refused at – guess – the eleventh.

By the beginning of the 1937–8 season Golden Miller was still only ten, but his powers were on the wane, and in the 1938 Gold Cup – ridden by Frenchie Nicholson, father of David – he had to accept the runner-up berth, two lengths behind Morse Code. It was the only time Golden Miller was beaten at Cheltenham.

Spared another disagreement with the eleventh fence in the National, Golden Miller ran just once more, in a handicap chase at Newbury nearly a year after his last Gold Cup. He finished unplaced, and was not asked to race again. With Insurance as his companion, he spent his retirement at Miss Paget's Elsenham Stud in Essex, where he was put down in January 1957 after suffering a heart attack.

Mill Reef

bay colt by Never Bend out of Milan Mill
1968–1986 (raced 1970–1972)
ran 14 races; won 12

Mill Reef, bred in the United States by his owner Paul Mellon and trained in England by Ian Balding, graced European racing with a virtually unbroken sequence of outstanding performances in his three seasons on the track, ridden throughout by Geoff Lewis.

His two-year-old season in 1970 yielded five wins from six outings, including wide-margin victories in the Coventry Stakes at Royal Ascot (eight lengths), Gimcrack Stakes at York (ten lengths) and Dewhurst Stakes at Newmarket (four lengths). The only blot was a short-head defeat by the brilliant My Swallow in the Prix Robert Papin at Maisons-Laffitte.

Mill Reef was the only horse to have won the Derby, King George VI and Queen Elizabeth Stakes and Prix de l'Arc de Triomphe in the same season until Lammtarra repeated the feat in 1995.

At three he took the Greenham Stakes at Newbury en route to the famous Two Thousand Guineas which pitted him against Brigadier Gerard and My Swallow: the resulting defeat by three lengths at the hands of 'The Brigadier' was the last he would ever experience. He took the Derby from Linden Tree, the Eclipse Stakes from Caro and the King George VI and Queen Elizabeth Stakes from Ortis, and brought his brilliant three-year-old term to a glorious close with a three-length victory over Pistol Packer in the Prix de l'Arc de Triomphe.

The same breathtaking acceleration was on display again in Mill Reef's first race at four, the Prix Ganay at Longchamp, taking him ten lengths clear by the line, but in the Coronation Cup he had to plug on dourly to get home just a neck from Homeric, raising fears that all was not well with the horse. Whatever it was, Mill Reef was not to delight the racegoing public again: on 30 August 1972 he fractured a foreleg on the gallops. Happily, a combination of veterinary brilliance and equine stoicism saved him for a highly successful stud career, and among the offspring he sired at the National Stud were Shirley Heights, winner of the 1978 Derby and himself sire of a Derby winner in Slip Anchor (1985), Acamas (Prix du Jockey-Club, 1978), Fairy Footsteps (One Thousand Guineas, 1981), Wassl (Irish Two Thousand Guineas, 1983) and Reference Point (Derby, King George and St Leger, 1987). He was put down in early 1986 at the age of eighteen on account of a deteriorating heart condition.

John Oaksey described the moment of truth of the 1971 Prix de l'Arc de Triomphe in his book *The Story of Mill Reef*. After turning for home, his hero is in danger of getting boxed in – and then a gap appears.

It can't have been very wide and it certainly would not have stayed open very long. But for Mill Reef at this, the climax of his whole career, it was enough. One moment we were searching anxiously along the jumbled line of colours, the next they parted and, like some projectile thrown from an angry crowd, a small, dark, utterly unmistakable figure detached itself.

For what happened in the next twenty seconds or so I have had to rely on films and photographs because at the time the Press Box, full of supposedly hard-headed scribes, exploded into something very like hysteria. It is never easy at the best of times to analyse a finish while screaming your head off, and even harder when a large French lady is waving her parasol under your nose . . .

Nijinsky

bay colt by Northern Dancer out of Flaming Page
1967–1992 (raced 1969–1970)
ran 13 races; won 11

'You couldn't help falling in love with Nijinsky as soon as you saw him.' The opinion not of some sentimental horse-lover but of the normally taciturn and unemotional Lester Piggott speaks volumes for the magic of the horse whose greatest highs and lows he shared. Nijinsky was the last horse to win the Triple Crown of Two Thousand Guineas, Derby and St Leger, and the first to achieve that feat since Bahram in 1935.

A son of Northern Dancer, Nijinsky was bought as a yearling in Canada for $84,000 by Charles Engelhard and sent to Vincent O'Brien in Ireland. Despite proving a difficult youngster – a fussy eater, and none too keen on the routine of being trained – he won all five of his races at two: four in Ireland, then a facile success in the Dewhurst Stakes at Newmarket.

A statue of Nijinsky was unveiled at The Curragh by Vincent O'Brien in October 1998.

The three-year-old career which was to make Nijinsky a legend opened at The Curragh in April 1970 with victory over the four-year-old Deep Run, soon to become the most influential National Hunt sire of all. The Two Thousand Guineas delivered up an easy win from Yellow God; then came the Derby. At Epsom, in the face of uncertainty about his ability to cope with the nerve-racking prelims, act on the course and stay the trip, let alone beat the high-class French challenger Gyr, Nijinsky started odds against for the only time in his racing life. No worries: Nijinsky and Lester swept past Gyr in the closing stages, and a true star was born. Next came a simple win over Meadowville in the Irish Derby and a first meeting with older horses in the King George at Ascot, where Nijinsky toyed with the opposition, headed by the previous year's Derby winner Blakeney.

The Triple Crown beckoned, but an attack of American ringworm severely debilitated the horse before the St Leger, and he arrived at Doncaster at less than his peak – not that you'd have known that from the race, in which Nijinsky sauntered into the record books, winning hard held from Meadowville.

Claiming the Triple Crown was a mammoth achievement, but there was more on Nijinsky's itinerary. In October 1970 he went to Longchamp to set the seal on a wonderful career in the Arc, but veered away from the whip in a fierce tussle with Sassafras and went down by a head. This was a crushing disappointment, but Nijinsky could not be allowed to bow out a losing note, and thirteen days after the Arc he was out again – at Newmarket for the Champion Stakes. The huge and adoring crowd that day reduced Nijinsky to a nervous wreck and he completely failed to run to his best, finishing a deeply disappointing second to Lorenzaccio.

Nijinsky was retired to stud at the Claiborne Farm in Kentucky, and by the time of his death in 1992 had sired many top-class horses, including Derby winners Golden Fleece (1982) and Shahrastani (1986) – with Lammtarra (1995) adding a third Derby posthumously. Two other Derby winners – Kahyasi (1988) and Generous (1991) – are grandsons of Nijinsky.

Lester Piggott again: 'Nijinsky possessed more natural ability than any horse I ever rode, before or since. It all seemed so easy for him . . . He was probably as good at two as he ever was – which is the case with many big horses – but during the summer of his three-year-old career, and especially in his Derby and King George, he was one of the greats.'

One Man

grey gelding by Remainder Man out of Steal On
1988–1998 (raced 1992–1998)
ran 35 races; won 20

The death of One Man in the Mumm Melling Chase at Aintree on 3 April 1998 cast a shadow not only over the Grand National meeting but over the whole of the 1997–8 jumps season. Not since the demise of Dawn Run in 1986 had such a popular horse been killed in action.

Like so many other great chasers, One Man was bred in Ireland; sold for 4,000 Irish guineas as an unbroken three-year-old, he made his racing debut in an Irish point-to-point where he distinguished himself by running out. He then went into training in Bishop Auckland, County Durham, with Arthur Stephenson, and at the dispersal sale in May 1993 following Stephenson's death was sold for 68,000 guineas to toy manufacturer John Hales and sent to the late Gordon Richards's yard. He won three novice hurdles, but really came into his own when put over fences, running up a sequence of five wins in 1993–4 before disappointing in the Sun Alliance Chase at Cheltenham.

The following season he announced his arrival in the top bracket with a convincing win in the Hennessy Cognac Gold Cup at Newbury, but failed to complete on two subsequent outings. The 1995 King George VI Chase was relocated to Sandown Park after the Kempton Boxing Day fixture had succumbed to the weather, but the change made no difference to One Man, who under Richard Dunwoody produced a display of dazzling authority to leave Monsieur Le Cure and Master Oats toiling in his wake as he powered up the Sandown hill.

One Man now became a very warm order for the Cheltenham Gold Cup, and despite doubts about his stamina over the longer trip started

11–8 favourite. Coming down the hill he looked to be well in contention, but after the entrance to the straight he folded in a matter of strides, barely managed to clamber over the final fence and finished a desperately tired sixth behind Imperial Call.

A year later he was back for another crack, having easily won a second King George (safely restored to Kempton on Boxing Day 1996) in record time to invite inevitable comparisons with another dashing grey who excelled at the Sunbury track: Desert Orchid. But his running in the 1997 Gold Cup was uncannily similar to the previous year's: after closing on Mr Mulligan between the last two fences he went out like a light and again finished sixth. Now not only One Man's stamina was being called into question, but his resolution: was he ducking the issue?

One Man's first two outings in the 1997–8 term saw him sticking to his guns well enough when beating Barton Bank at Wetherby and Viking Flagship at Huntingdon, but he then seemed to lose his way again: in the race he was beginning to make his own, the King George, toiling in the rain-softened ground, he could finish only fifth behind See More Business. Next stop Ascot, for a facile win, then it was back to Cheltenham – not for the Gold Cup this time but to make a pitch for the two-mile title, the Queen Mother Champion Chase. Deserted by Richard Dunwoody and now ridden by Brian Harding, who had partnered the horse in much of his work at home, One Man produced a fluent display of jumping that kept him in the vanguard throughout, and as the field came down the hill the same old question nagged: would he collapse again? The answer was an emphatic negative. One Man was not stopping, and to whoops of joy from the crowd he soared over the last and set off up the hill to beat Or Royal. It was one of the great Cheltenham moments.

The clash at Aintree between One Man and Strong Promise – who had run a marvellous race to finish second in the Gold Cup – was keenly anticipated. Swinging out down the back straight One Man was leading and well in command, but at the ninth fence he seemed to jink to the right and lunge at the obstacle, taking a very heavy fall and breaking a tibia. He was put down immediately.

Timeform's *Chasers and Hurdlers* succinctly captured the contrasting moods of One Man's last two races: 'It is very hard to imagine this sport experiencing anything better or anything worse.'

Pretty Polly

chestnut mare by Gallinule out of Admiration
1901–1931 (raced 1903–1906)
ran 24 races; won 22

One of the greatest racemares in English racing history and the idol of contemporary racegoers, Pretty Polly was foaled near The Curragh at the stud of her breeder Major Eustace Loder, who sent her to Newmarket trainer Peter Purcell Gilpin.

She won her first race as a two-year-old at Sandown Park by ten lengths, returned to that course to win the prestigious National Breeders Produce Stakes, started at 33–1 on for her next race (which she won) and ended her juvenile career unbeaten in nine outings, including the Champagne Stakes at Doncaster and the Cheveley Park Stakes and Middle Park Plate (precursor of today's Middle Park Stakes) at Newmarket.

Pretty Polly's starting price of 100–8 on in the 1904 Oaks was the shortest ever returned in an English Classic.

Her three-year-old debut came in the One Thousand Guineas, which she won easily. At Epsom she beat three rivals to take the Oaks at 100–8 on. She then won the Coronation Stakes at Royal Ascot and the Nassau Stakes at Goodwood before going to Doncaster for the St Leger: starting at 5–2 on, she duly won, and for good measure took the Park Hill Stakes at the same meeting two days later.

Unbeaten and apparently unbeatable, Pretty Polly was sent over to Longchamp to put the best French horses in their place in the Prix du

Conseil Municipal. In heavy going which did not suit her and after a bad trip across the Channel, she was beaten by Presto II. The defeat caused a sensation; but at the end of October the beloved filly had found the winning thread again and took the Free Handicap at Newmarket despite bearing a burden of nine stone seven pounds. At last it was decided that she had done enough for 1904.

Pretty Polly went through her four-year-old career unbeaten, winning the Coronation Cup, Champion Stakes, Limekiln Stakes and Jockey Club Cup. She remained in training at five, but after winning the March Stakes at Newmarket and the Coronation Cup ended her career on quite the wrong note with a narrow defeat by Bachelor's Button in the Ascot Gold Cup. This was no time for impartiality, and the *Sporting Life* wore its heart on its sleeve: 'Alas, and again Alas! Pretty Polly beaten! Lamentations as sincere as they were loud were heard on every hand after the race was over.'

At stud Pretty Polly had limited success in the short term, but left a lasting mark as the ancestor of such horses as consecutive Derby winners Psidium and St Paddy, and as great-great-great-granddam of Brigadier Gerard. She was put down at the age of thirty in 1931.

Red Rum

bay gelding by Quorum out of Mared
1965–1995 (raced 1967–1978)
ran 110 races; won 27

Red Rum has a secure place in racing history. He was – and most probably will remain – the only horse ever to have won the Grand National three times.

Born in County Kilkenny, Red Rum was sold as a yearling for 400 guineas to trainer and former champion jump jockey Tim Molony. His first race was a two-year-old selling plate at Liverpool in April 1967, the day before the famous Foinavon Grand National: ridden by Paul Cook, Red Rum dead-heated for first place with Curlicue. There were to be nine more runs on the Flat for this future jumping hero, and two of them he won outright.

Over the course of his racing career Red Rum passed through the hands of no fewer than five trainers: Tim Molony, Bobby Renton, Tommy Stack, Tony Gillam and Ginger McCain.

Sold on to Mrs Lurline Brotherton (who had owned 1950 Grand National winner Freebooter), Red Rum was briefly trained by Tommy Stack, who would re-enter his story for its greatest moment. Although he won over hurdles and fences his racing potential was clouded by the foot disease pedal ostitis, and in August 1972 he was bought at the Doncaster Sales for 6,000 guineas on behalf of millionaire Noel Le Mare by Donald – 'Ginger' – McCain, who combined training race-horses with his second-hand car business in Southport, Lancashire.

The move to the coast transformed Red Rum. Being trained on the sands and galloping through the sea worked wonders on his foot problems, and by Grand National day 1973 he had become one of the leading staying chasers in the north – so good that he started 9–1 joint favourite for the National alongside the top weight, the great Australian chaser Crisp.

Red Rum, ridden by Brian Fletcher, did not endear himself to every racing fan that day, catching Crisp just short of the winning post after the Australian horse had built up a huge lead and put up the bravest front-running performance ever seen in the National. Receiving twenty-three pounds from Crisp, the winner got home by three-quarters of a length in a time which demolished the course record; and the majority of observers thought it a cruel injustice that the front-runner had not held on. That said, Red Rum had shown great persistence as Crisp's only serious pursuer, and great agility and economy jumping the Aintree fences.

After their epic Grand National in 1973, Red Rum and Crisp met again in a two-horse race at Doncaster the following November. They started at level weights, and Crisp won effortlessly by eight lengths.

A year later, with Crisp sidelined, Red Rum galloped home from L'Escargot to become the first dual National winner for nearly forty years. That year he himself carried top weight of twelve stone, and three weeks later went on to win the Scottish National under eleven stone thirteen pounds to prove himself an exceptional horse.

Red Rum showed good form away from Liverpool – he was beaten only a short head in the 1973 Hennessy Gold Cup at Newbury – but saved his best for the Grand National, and, after finishing runner-up to L'Escargot in 1975 and Rag Trade in 1976, lined up for his fifth con-secutive National in 1977. Tommy Stack, formerly his trainer, was now his established jockey, and despite the horse's advancing years – he was now twelve – Red Rum was strongly fancied for a unique third win in the race: he started at 9–1. After front-runner Andy Pandy had fallen at second Becher's there was only going to be one winner, and over the last two fences Red Rum shook off the challenge of Churchtown Boy to romp home by twenty-five lengths, as the crowd went wild and Peter O'Sullevan delivered one of his most famous commentaries: 'He's coming up to the line, to win it like a fresh horse in great style. It's hats off and a tremendous reception – you've never heard one like it at Liverpool!'

It was to be Red Rum's last run in the race. In 1978 he was being prepared for his sixth National when on the eve of the big day a leg injury ruled him out, and he was retired – from racing, but not from public appearances: for years thereafter Red Rum, a genuine equine celebrity and the first British racehorse whose commercial potential was seriously tapped, was a familiar sight opening betting shops or leading the Grand National parade. He was a star, and brought jump racing – and the Grand National in particular – to a wider public than it had previously attracted.

Red Rum's particular qualities as a Grand National horse were his balance and cleverness: never a flamboyant jumper, he was nimble enough to swerve out of trouble and keep up his relentless gallop.

He died in 1995 at the age of thirty and is now buried – where else? – by the winning post at Aintree.

Lester Piggott rode Red Rum in the Earl of Sefton's Stakes at Liverpool in March 1968: they were beaten a short head.

Ribot

bay colt by Tenerani out of Romanella
1952–1972 (raced 1954–1956)
ran 16 races; won 16

Unbeaten in all of his sixteen races, Ribot was the greatest Italian-trained racehorse of the century.

Bred by the Marchese Incisa della Rochetta and the great Italian breeder Federico Tesio (who died before the colt ever raced), Ribot was foaled in 1952 at the English National Stud, and went into training in Italy with Ugo Penco. As a two-year-old and three-year-old he won seven races without experiencing defeat, but Italy could not muster sufficiently stiff opposition to test the horse fully, and in the autumn of 1955 he travelled to Paris for the Arc, his first race outside his home country. His reputation had preceded him but he started at almost 9–1 before being steered home by his regular jockey Enrico Camici to win by three lengths from Beau Prince II. He then won one more race in Italy to bring his score by the end of 1955 to nine out of nine.

As a four-year-old in 1956 Ribot came to England for the only time in his career, defying soggy going to land the King George VI and Queen Elizabeth Stakes at Ascot, beating High Veldt by five lengths. Later that year he returned to Longchamp for a second Arc and, in what was to be his final race, won by six lengths from Irish Derby winner Talgo.

Ribot stood as a stallion for one year in England before moving to Italy and then to the United States, where he remained until his death in 1972: it had been the intention to return him to Europe, but the horse had become very difficult to manage and the idea of undertaking such a journey was vetoed. Among Ribot's offspring were Arc winners Molvedo and Prince Royal II, and English Classic winners Ribocco, Ribero, Ragusa, Long Look and Boucher.

Sceptre

bay mare by Persimmon out of Ornament
1899–1926 (raced 1901–1904)
ran 25 races; won 13

No horse has ever won all five English Classics, but Sceptre came the closest. In 1902 she won the Two Thousand Guineas, One Thousand Guineas, Oaks and St Leger and finished fourth in the Derby, and by any standards must be ranked not only one of the all-time greats, but one of the toughest racemares ever.

Bred in the purple by the 1st Duke of Westminster – her dam was a full sister to the great horse Ormonde – Sceptre was sold by public auction following the Duke's death in 1899 and bought for 10,000 guineas, a massive amount at the time, by Robert Sievier, a notorious gambler.

As a two-year-old she won the Woodcote Stakes at Epsom and the July Stakes at Newmarket before coming third in the Champagne Stakes at Doncaster, but at the end of that season her trainer Charles Morton became private trainer to J. B. Joel, and Sievier decided to train his filly himself. Although well aware that he had a Classic filly on his hands, Sievier could not resist a gamble, and Sceptre's first race as a three-year-old in 1902 was the Lincoln Handicap: overtrained by Sievier's assistant, Sceptre was beaten by the four-year-old St Maclou.

Despite that reverse, she thrived physically thereafter, and by the time of the Two Thousand Guineas was at her peak. She won the first Classic in record time and followed up two days later in the One Thousand despite losing a shoe at the start. In the Derby she started even-money favourite but could only finish fourth behind Ard Patrick, and yet after just one day's rest came out again to win the Oaks.

Between the Oaks and St Leger, Sceptre's schedule ran as follows:

Grand Prix de Paris (beaten); Coronation Stakes at Royal Ascot (beaten); the following day the St James's Palace Stakes (won); Sussex Stakes at Goodwood (beaten); Nassau Stakes (won). No wonder she looked worn out by the time of the St Leger – but she won the final Classic by three lengths to claim a unique place in British racing history.

Relko in 1963 was the first descendant of Sceptre in the direct female line to win the Derby.

Surely no horse ever deserved a rest more; but two days after The Leger poor Sceptre was out again – to be beaten in the Park Hill Stakes.

Her four-year-old season in 1903 again began in the Lincoln: this time she could finish only fifth, and following the race was sold to provide some temporary alleviation of Sievier's chronic financial problems. Her new owner, William Bass, sent her to the great trainer Alec Taylor at Manton, and gradually she started to thrive once more. She won the Hardwicke Stakes at Royal Ascot and then played a leading role in one of the greatest races ever, beaten a neck in the Eclipse Stakes by Ard Patrick, the horse who had won the Derby in her year, with 1903 Derby winner Rock Sand third. That autumn Sceptre not only won the Champion Stakes but beat Rock Sand – by then winner of the Triple Crown – to land the Jockey Club Stakes.

As a five-year-old she failed to run up to her best – who could blame her? – and was beaten in the Coronation Cup, Ascot Gold Cup and Hardwicke Stakes.

At stud she bred four winners but was somewhat disappointing. She died in 1926.

Sea Bird II

chestnut colt by Dan Cupid out of Sicalade
1962–1973 (raced 1964–1965)
ran 8 races; won 7

Although Sea Bird II ran just eight races in his life, and only one of them in England, there is no serious disputing that he was the very best horse to have run on the Flat in Europe since the Second World War, nor that he was one of the all-time greats. He may not have pleased purist paddock-watchers – he was a bright chestnut with a thin white blaze, two white stockings and an excitable temperament – but could he gallop!

Sea Bird was bred in France by his owner M. Jean Ternynck and trained at Chantilly by Etienne Pollet. Although his sire Dan Cupid was a son of the great American horse Native Dancer, his dam Sicalade came from humbler stock – so humble that she was sold for the equivalent of £100 for butcher's meat before her illustrious son ever raced.

In three outings as a two-year-old, Sea Bird won twice and was then beaten in the Grand Criterium at Longchamp by his stable companion Grey Dawn – but he was never beaten again.

Sea Bird opened his three-year-old campaign with a facile victory in the Prix Greffulhe at Longchamp, following up with a six-length rout of Diatome in the Prix Lupin at the same course. Sights were then set on the Derby at Epsom, for the only occasion on which the horse would race beyond his native shores. Starting hot favourite at 7–4 and ridden by Australian jockey Pat Glennon, Sea Bird hacked up at Epsom, sweeping into the lead hard held inside the final furlong to become one of the easiest Derby winners ever. His margin over Meadow Court may have been a mere two lengths, but Sea Bird had never come off the bridle to achieve it. Indeed, Glennon subsequently reported that his only worry during the race was how to pull up his mount beyond the winning post!

His reputation as a racehorse of exceptional merit secured, Sea Bird then won the Grand Prix de Saint-Cloud, after which it was announced that the Prix de l'Arc de Triomphe would be his last race.

That 1965 Arc saw one of the best fields ever assembled for any horse race, including Derby runner-up Meadow Court, who since his defeat at Epsom had won the Irish Derby and the King George VI and Queen Elizabeth Stakes at Ascot; Reliance II, winner of the Prix du Jockey-Club and the second best three-year-old in France; Diatome, runner-up in the Prix du Jockey-Club and later that year winner of the Washington International; Anilin, the best horse in Russia; and the American challenger Tom Rolfe, winner of the Preakness Stakes.

It all boiled down to a duel up the Longchamp straight between Reliance and Sea Bird – and while Reliance was a great horse, Sea Bird was a superlative one. The two came clear of their rivals, then Sea Bird just surged away, veering to the outside of the track but still recording a six-length verdict over Reliance, who was himself five lengths ahead of the third horse Diatome. It was a monumental performance, a race against which lesser horses would have to be judged.

Sea Bird II stood as a stallion in the United States for five years before returning to France, where he died in 1973. He achieved little at stud to compare with his supremacy as a racehorse, though his offspring included the very good French colt Gyr, second to Nijinsky in the 1970 Derby, and two great favourites: Allez France, winner of the Arc in 1974, and Sea Pigeon, dual Champion Hurdler in 1980 and 1981 (see overleaf).

Sea Bird II earned the highest rating on the Flat ever awarded by Timeform. The top five ratings to the end of 1998, expressed in pounds in similar fashion to official ratings, were:

145 Sea Bird II (1965)
144 Brigadier Gerard (1972), Tudor Minstrel (1947)
142 Abernant (1950), Windy City (1951), Ribot (1956)
141 Mill Reef (1972)
140 Vaguely Noble (1968), Shergar (1981), Dancing Brave (1986)

Sea Pigeon

brown gelding by Sea Bird II out of Around The Roses
1970– (raced 1972–1981)
ran 85 races; won 37

One of only two horses to have won the Champion Hurdle at the advanced age of eleven, Sea Pigeon was bred to be a high-class performer on the Flat. His one race as a two-year-old in 1972, in which he won the Duke of Edinburgh Stakes at Ascot, did nothing to dispel the hopes of owner–breeder Jock Whitney and trainer Jeremy Tree that the colt had Classic pretensions, but although Sea Pigeon did get to the Derby line-up in 1973, in the event he could finish only seventh behind Morston. After failing to win at all as a three-year-old, the colt was gelded and subsequently sold to Pat Muldoon, for whom he was trained by first Gordon Richards and later Peter Easterby.

In a hurdling career which began at Newcastle in November 1974 and ended at the same course in November 1981, Sea Pigeon won twenty-one of his forty starts, and ran in five consecutive runnings of the Champion Hurdle. Fourth behind Night Nurse in 1977, he returned to Cheltenham a year later for the first of his series of titanic Champion Hurdle duels with Monksfield. Three years running the pair came to the last flight locked together. In 1978 Monksfield asserted up the run-in and won by two lengths; in 1979 the two had a desperate duel from the last before Monksfield again got the upper hand to win by three-quarters of a length; but in 1980 Sea Pigeon finally managed to turn the tables, going clear of his rival to win by seven lengths under Jonjo O'Neill.

By the time of the 1981 running Monksfield had been retired. John Francome, who had come in for the ride on the eleven-year-old Sea

Pigeon as Jonjo had been sidelined through injury, presented the Cheltenham crowd with a typical piece of artistry. Sea Pigeon was a horse who tended to idle in front and needed producing at the very last minute, so John let Daring Run and Pollardstown lead over the last before easing past them inside the last hundred yards to win cosily – a riding performance of exceptional cool-headedness.

At the time of his retirement Sea Pigeon had won more prize money than any other horse under National Hunt Rules.

In addition to his two Champion Hurdles, Sea Pigeon won many other big races over jumps, including the Scottish Champion Hurdle at Ayr twice, the Welsh Champion Hurdle at Chepstow and the Fighting Fifth Hurdle at Newcastle twice. It was undoubtedly a great record; but the root of Sea Pigeon's appeal was his versatility, and a distinguished Flat career was being played out in parallel with the winter game. Sea Pigeon won the Chester Cup twice, the Vaux Gold Tankard at Redcar three times, the Moët and Chandon Silver Magnum for amateur riders at Epsom and the Doonside Cup at Ayr – but his greatest moment on the level was winning the 1979 Ebor Handicap at York. Ridden by Jonjo O'Neill and carrying the crushing burden of ten stone (the highest weight carried to victory in the famous handicap this century), Sea Pigeon won by a short head from Donegal Prince.

One of the most popular racehorses ever to have graced the sport, Sea Pigeon was retired shortly before the 1982 Champion Hurdle and at the time of writing is enjoying his leisure in Yorkshire.

Secretariat

chestnut colt by Bold Ruler out of Somethingroyal
1970–1989 (raced 1972–1973)
ran 21 races; won 16

'Wow!'

The word that Penny Tweedy, manager of Meadow Stud in Virginia, entered in her notebook on first seeing a big chestnut colt foal with three white feet was to be uttered a million times during that horse's racing career. No question: Secretariat, winner of the US Triple Crown in 1973, was one of the all-time greats.

Trained by Lucien Laurin, Secretariat first ran as a two-year-old in July 1972, finishing fourth, then proceeded to win his next eight races (though he was disqualified after one) and was voted Horse of the Year.

'He could not have moved faster if he had fallen off the grandstand roof' – American racing writer Charlie Hatton on Secretariat in the Belmont Stakes.

His three-year-old career in 1973 kicked off with two easy victories; then there was a defeat (reason: infected boil in his mouth); then it was off to the Kentucky Derby at Churchill Downs, first leg of the Triple Crown. Secretariat smashed Northern Dancer's course record when winning the 'Run for the Roses' from Sham, then despatched the same horse in the second leg, the Preakness Stakes at Pimlico (again breaking the track record).

Two down, one to go – and Secretariat was already a national hero, a welcome distraction from the unfolding saga of Watergate. The Triple

Crown had not been won since Citation had achieved the feat a quarter of a century earlier in 1948, but Secretariat looked a shoo-in for the final leg, the Belmont Stakes over one and a half miles, and started 10–1 on favourite. A crowd of 70,000 crammed into Belmont Park to see 'Big Red' on his date with destiny, and few of them expected him to lose; but fewer still could have expected what they were to witness – possibly the greatest individual performance in racing history.

Ridden by Ron Turcotte, Secretariat shot out of the starting gate from his inside berth and set out to make all, with Sham trying to take issue. They passed the stands at a searing pace and swung round the clubhouse turn, drawing a gasp from the crowd as the time for the first quarter was posted: 23.6 seconds, a breakneck pace for such a long race. Down the back straight Sham fell away, leaving Secretariat in glorious isolation. After a mile had been run the chestnut was seven lengths ahead, and his lead was still building rapidly – so rapidly that he was over twenty lengths clear by the turn into the home stretch. The crowd went wild as Secretariat barrelled home, and at the wire the winning margin from Twice A Prince was an astonishing thirty-one lengths – and another course time had been shattered. An astounding performance.

Secretariat ran six more times, winning four, including the Arlington Invitational, the Man O'War Stakes (on grass) and the Canadian International Turf Championship. He was then retired to Claiborne Farm in Kentucky, where he died in 1989 at the age of nineteen.

A mark of the magnitude of Secretariat's performance in the 1973 Belmont Stakes is that 5,617 winning on-course tote tickets for that race – value $14,597 – were not cashed in. Punters were keeping them as mementoes of an unrepeatable occasion.

Shergar

bay colt by Great Nephew out of Sharmeen
1978–1983 (raced 1980–1981)
ran 8 races; won 6

It is Shergar's fate to be remembered less for his glittering racing career than for what befell him after he had retired from the track. On the night of 8 February 1983, shortly before his second season standing as a stallion, he was abducted from the Aga Khan's Ballymany Stud, just outside Newbridge near The Curragh in County Kildare, and never heard of again. Ransom demands from his kidnappers – widely assumed to be the IRA on a fund-raising drive – drew no response, and it is assumed that the horse was killed a few days after his kidnapping.

Twelve days after the 1981 Derby, during his preparations for the Irish Derby, Shergar got loose on Newmarket Heath and ran free until being caught by a van driver outside Henry Cecil's Warren Place stables at the top of Warren Hill.

If Shergar's end was tragic, his brief period on the racecourse was epic.

Bred by his owner the Aga Khan and trained by Michael Stoute, Shergar raced just twice as a two-year-old, winning at Newbury and then finishing runner-up to Beldale Flutter in the William Hill Futurity (now the Racing Post Trophy) at Doncaster. A promising start, but it was his first appearance at three which really raised eyebrows – a ten-length victory in the Guardian Classic Trial at Sandown Park. The previous three runnings of the Classic Trial had thrown up the winner of the Derby – Shirley Heights had run second in 1978, then Troy and Henbit had each won the Sandown race – and Shergar's victory made him a serious Epsom candidate, a position which solidified after he had won the Chester Vase by twelve lengths. Such was the impression which Shergar made in these two races that after Chester the late Richard Baerlein of the *Observer* famously observed of Shergar's chance in the Derby: 'Now is the time to bet like men.'

Not for a moment on Derby Day did Richard Baerlein seem likely to be proved wrong. Ridden by nineteen-year-old Walter Swinburn having his first ride in the premier Classic, Shergar was cantering all over his rivals for the first half of the race, then eased his way to the front soon after entering the straight and scampered clear of Glint Of Gold for a ten-length victory – the longest winning distance ever in the Derby.

Next came the Irish Derby. Walter Swinburn was suspended, so Lester Piggott (who had ridden the colt in both his two-year-old races) came in for an armchair spare ride. The pair won unchallenged by four lengths, but it was the manner of the victory which made it memorable: Shergar passed his rivals in a hack canter to win with ridiculous ease. No three-year-old could get near him, so it was time to face older horses such as Master Willie and Light Cavalry in the King George VI and Queen Elizabeth Diamond Stakes at Ascot. Here too Shergar won easily, by four lengths from Madam Gay.

He then had a rest until the St Leger, expected to be a doddle en route to Paris for the Arc. Instead, it was a disaster: Shergar failed to show his true spark at Doncaster and faded in the final quarter of a mile to finish a labouring fourth behind Cut Above. Arc plans were shelved, and he did not race again. His career had consisted of eight races.

Shergar had just one season at stud – too little time to assess his long-term potential as a stallion – before the IRA came for him that February night.

Winners and losers

HORSE SENSE from John McCririck

As Channel Four Racing's resident expert on the subject, FAT has to be my watchword when eyeing up a horse. No matter what its form figures, if the creature looks grotesquely obese, just like what I do, forget it!

On the plus side, go for a horse with big ears – like that great old handicapper Loppylugs, who won the Cambridgeshire back in 1956: he wore blinkers but was as game as they come. Myself and Prince Charles also qualify.

When a horse is on its toes, fine. But if it is sweating or the handler is constantly tugging at the reins, the beast, like a greyhound straining on the leash, is wasting precious nervous energy and should be treated cautiously.

Of horses we've seen in recent years, Zafonic was quite magnificent. In size, conformation and sheer quality, he simply dominated his rivals – in the paddock as in the race.

And here's a short cut to finding your pick of the parade ring. Imagine all the horses were set loose and stampeded up the racecourse. Which one, by its very presence, physically and mentally, would emerge as the leader?

Winners and losers

You win some, you lose some – and some horses win more (and lose more) than others . . .

- Kincsem, an Austro-Hungarian filly foaled in 1874, was unbeaten in 54 races, including the Goodwood Cup in 1878.

- Other famous unblemished careers include Eclipse (18 wins), Ribot (16 wins) and Ormonde (16 wins).

- Record for the most wins in a career is held by Galgo Jr., a Puerto Rican horse who between 1930 and 1936 won 137 of his 159 races.

- Another Puerto Rican horse, Camerero, set the world record of 56 consecutive wins between 1953 and 1955 – the first 56 runs of his career. In all he won 73 of his 77 races.

- Career record for a British-bred horse is held by Catherina, who raced between 1832 and 1841: 79 wins from 176 starts.

- British record for wins in one season is held by Fisherman: 23 in 1856.

- Crudwell was the last horse to win 50 races in Britain – 7 on the Flat, 4 over hurdles and 39 steeplechases, including the Welsh Grand National (ridden by Dick Francis) in 1956. His first victory was over twelve furlongs at Leicester in March 1950, his fiftieth at Wincanton on 15 September 1960 when, ridden by Michael Scudamore (father of Peter), he won the Somerset Chase at the age of fourteen. He did not race again.

- Good old Further Flight is the only horse to have won the same Pattern race five years in a row: he won the Jockey Club Cup at Newmarket every year from 1991 to 1995.

- Fifteen horses have won the English Triple Crown of Two Thousand Guineas, Derby and St Leger: West Australian (1853), Gladiateur (1865), Lord Lyon (1866), Ormonde (1886), Common (1891), Isinglass (1893), Galtee More (1897), Flying Fox (1899), Diamond Jubilee (1900), Rock Sand (1903), Pommern (1915), Gay Crusader (1917), Gainsborough (1918), Bahram (1935) and Nijinsky (1970).

- Seven fillies have won the Fillies' Triple Crown of One Thousand Guineas, Oaks and St Leger: Hannah (1871), Apology (1874), La Fleche (1892), Pretty Polly (1904), Sun Chariot (1942), Meld (1955) and Oh So Sharp (1985).

- Only Sceptre (see page 138) has won four English Classics outright: Two Thousand Guineas, One Thousand Guineas, Oaks and St Leger in 1902. Formosa in 1868 won the One Thousand Guineas, Oaks and St Leger outright and dead-heated in the Two Thousand Guineas.

- Eleven horses have won the American Triple Crown of Kentucky Derby, Preakness Stakes and Belmont Stakes: Sir Barton (1919), Gallant Fox (1930), Omaha (1935), War Admiral (1937), Whirlaway (1941), Count Fleet (1943), Assault (1946), Citation (1948), Secretariat (1973), Seattle Slew (1977) and Affirmed (1978).

- L'Escargot is the only horse apart from Golden Miller to have won the Cheltenham Gold Cup (1970 and 1971) and Grand National (1975).

A select band of horses have scored three or more wins in the major jumping races:

- Grand National: three times, Red Rum (1973, 1974, 1977);
- Cheltenham Gold Cup: five times, Golden Miller (1932, 1933, 1934, 1935, 1936); three times, Cottage Rake (1948, 1949, 1950), Arkle (1964, 1965, 1966);
- Champion Hurdle: three times, Hatton's Grace (1949, 1950, 1951), Sir Ken (1952, 1953, 1954), Persian War (1968, 1969, 1970), See You Then (1985, 1986, 1987);
- Queen Mother Champion Chase: three times, Badsworth Boy (1983, 1984, 1985);
- King George VI Chase: four times, Desert Orchid (1986, 1988, 1989, 1990); three times, Wayward Lad (1982, 1983, 1985).

That's enough winners. Now for the losers, beginning with a couple of honourable runners-up:

- Wyndburgh was second three times in the Grand National – 1957, 1959 and 1962.

- Alydar was second to Affirmed in all three legs of the American Triple Crown in 1977, and by ever-diminishing margins – beaten one and a half lengths in the Kentucky Derby, a neck in the Preakness, and a head in the Belmont.

- A maiden is a horse which has never won a race, but failing to get his head in front doesn't mean that he can't earn his keep. Needle Gun, trained by Clive Brittain, had earned £257,717 in place money from thirteen outings before finally losing his maiden tag in a minor race at Yarmouth in October 1994.

And then some less honourable:

- Rossa Prince and Mister Chippendale share the extremely dubious distinction of having failed to win a walkover. Both achieved this signal feat in point-to-points: in May 1990 Rossa Prince bolted while being saddled and could not be caught in time to meet the demands of the regulations, and in April 1994 Mister Chippendale forfeited his walkover prize when his rider omitted to weigh in.

- Black Humour has the rare distinction of having fallen in the Champion Hurdle (1991), Cheltenham Gold Cup (1993) and Grand National (1994).

- Amrullah failed to win in 74 races. He first ran in a two-year-old maiden race at Newmarket in October 1982, when he was unplaced behind Tolomeo, and last ran in a novices' chase at Fontwell Park in March 1992. Amrullah was placed often enough in good-class company to earn over £26,000 in prize money, but he just would not stir himself enough to win (the closest he came being defeat by a neck). Towards the end of his career he became something of a racing celebrity for the wrong reasons, but Timeform failed to see the joke, awarding him the dreaded 'double squiggle' as a mark of incorrigible unreliability and branding him 'thoroughly irresolute'.

- Amrullah's mantle as the loser people loved to cheer home was taken over later in the 1990s by Quixall Crossett. When running a very remote last to Suny Bay in the Tommy Whittle Chase at Haydock Park on 12 December 1998, Quixall Crossett was recording his eighty-first defeat from eighty-one races. If the problem with Amrullah was that he was thoroughly irresolute, Quixall Crossett's affliction was somewhat simpler: he was thoroughly slow – though earlier in 1998 he had given his supporters a scare when rallying to trouble the winner in a race at Wetherby. By New Year's Day 1999, Quixall Crossett – who is even more of a celebrity than was Amrullah – was up to eighty-two and still going . . . er . . . strong.

- The losing records of Amrullah and Quixall Crossett, impressive as they are, pale beside that of Peggy's Pet, who posted a career record of nought from ninety-four starts – Flat, hurdles and chases – between 1962 and 1970. He was also defeated in seventeen point-to-points.

- Yet even Peggy's Pet must give best to the Australian mare Oureone, who between 1976 and 1983 raced 124 times without winning.

- A comparative minnow in statistical terms but a major player in the 'worst horse ever to race in Britain' category is Elsich. The authorities pulled the plug in June 1947 after he had failed to win in fifty starts, and completed the course in only a third of these. In February 1945 he fell in two different races at Cheltenham on the same day. He ran three times in the Cheltenham Gold Cup, running out once, falling once and being pulled up once. He also fell at the first in the 1946 Grand National.

- And finally there's Zippy, the American horse whose attempts to keep a scorecard unsullied with victory caught the imagination of the United States. In September 1998, after his eighty-fifth consecutive defeat (a figure reached by two previous contenders who then spoiled everything by winning next time out), he was debarred from competing at his regular track, Finger Lakes in upstate New York: the stewards there announced they were banning him 'for the protection of the public'.

The international horse

HORSE SENSE from Alastair Down

What I look for in a horse has nothing to do with what a horse looks like! Handsome is as handsome does, and the holy grail I am after is a horse with the right attitude – the will to win and the inclination to scrap for it.

I would far rather own an ordinary horse that tries than a good one who doesn't. The most important thing for paddock judges to discern is fitness, but modern training methods – particularly over the jumps – mean that horses having their first run of the season are infinitely fitter than was the case twenty years ago. Fat horses palpably in need of the run were a commonplace then; now they are an exception.

Conformation gurus will wince at the swan-necked and parrot-mouthed, get the vapours about bad walkers, horses that dish their off-fore, are too straight in front or are just plain ordinary to look at. But believe me, if they have the mental attitude to compensate for the fact that they will never win a beauty contest they'll do for me. And no horse is perfect. The incomparable Arkle had the most wonderful head and what the poets would call the 'look of eagles', yet they say you could have driven a wheelbarrow through his back legs without any trouble. But you would have needed a 500cc wheelbarrow to catch up with him before you tried!

The international horse

With huge advances in air travel, horse racing has become increasingly international over the last two decades, to the extent that it is now common for horses based in Europe to make regular raids for the top prizes in far-flung corners of the globe – and very occasionally those far-flung corners send their own raiders to Europe.

The challengers

Racing on an international scale has come a long way since Papyrus, winner of the Derby in 1923, was sent in the autumn of that year to Belmont Park, New York, for a match with the top American horse Zev. Papyrus had to endure a lengthy sea crossing, was not given enough time to acclimatise once in the USA, and found himself singularly ill at ease in the conditions which prevailed at Belmont, where the dirt track had become a quagmire after prolonged rain. Zev won the match easily, and the idea of serious European challenges for American races was quietly forgotten for a quarter of a century.

It was the inauguration of the Washington International at Laurel Park, Maryland, in 1952 which paved the way for the regular transatlantic challenges we know today. That first running of the Washington International was won by Wilwyn, trained in England by George Colling and ridden by the late Manny Mercer, and by the end of the 1950s the race was often a target for top European horses looking to augment their domestic earnings with the huge prizes on offer in America. Ballymoss, winner in 1957 of the St Leger and Irish Derby and the following year of the Coronation Cup, Eclipse Stakes, King George and Prix de l'Arc de Triomphe, made a bid for the 1958 Washington International but after a rough passage in the race could finish only third. Ballymoss's trainer Vincent O'Brien and rider Lester Piggott did, however, win the Washington International ten years later, with Sir Ivor – in what turned out to be that great horse's final race – and a controversial affair it was too, with the American press slating Piggott for the sort of leave-it-to-the-last-second effort which British racegoers had long been applauding. Piggott won the International again on Karabas in 1969 and on the French-trained Argument in 1980.

The Washington International remained the principal US goal for European challengers until the Arlington Million was first run at Arlington Park, Chicago, in 1981. The inaugural running of the Million went to John Henry, but by the time this legendary American horse repeated the feat three years later the race had already gone for the first time to a British-trained runner, Luca Cumani's Tolomeo scooping the 1983 running at local odds of over 38–1 – tipped to do so by a visiting British journalist named Brough Scott! Two years later the popular gelding Teleprompter, trained in Yorkshire by Bill Watts, became – if only briefly – England's leading money-winner when winning the 1985 Arlington Million. (This feat also made him the first English-trained gelding to win a Group One or Grade One race anywhere in the world.)

Teleprompter's earnings record lasted only two months, for in November 1985 the brilliant filly Pebbles netted US$900,000 – £629,371 at the prevailing exchange rate – when landing the Breeders' Cup Turf at Aqueduct, New York.

That was the second running of the Breeders' Cup, a series of races for different types of horse over different distances and run each year at a different North American track, initiated at Hollywood Park, California, in 1984 with the intention that it should become a sort of world championship of horse racing. The Cup is now such an established part of the racing year that it is hard to remember the scepticism with which the idea was originally received in the early 1980s: when John Galbreath, American owner of 1972 Derby winner Roberto, heard of the scheme, he exclaimed to John Gaines, the famous breeder whose brainchild the event was, 'Why John, I didn't know you smoked pot!'

Gaines's vision was in fact brought about not by any mind-altering substance but by an acute commercial sense, and its self-proclaimed status as world championship has brought a host of memories for European contenders in the Cup's short life: Pebbles herself; Lester Piggott's victory on Royal Academy in the 1990 Mile twelve days after his comeback from retirement; Dayjur jumping the shadow in the Sprint the same day; Arazi's sensational slalom down the back stretch in the Juvenile in 1991; Miesque's back-to-back victories in the Mile in 1987 and 1988; Spinning World scorching away with the Mile in the same colours in 1997 ...

British-trained winners of Breeders' Cup races

The fifteen Breeders' Cups between 1984 and 1998 have yielded only four winners trained in Britain:

1985 Pebbles (Breeders' Cup Turf at Aqueduct, New York)
1991 Sheikh Albadou (Breeders' Cup Sprint at Churchill Downs, Kentucky)
1994 Barathea (Breeders' Cup Mile at Churchill Downs)
1996 Pilsudski (Breeders' Cup Turf at Woodbine, Toronto)

The reasons why British challengers find the Breeders' Cup races so difficult – stress of long-distance travel, need to acclimatise, different sorts of tracks, and so on – also account in part for why there have been so few European challengers for the three races which form the American Triple Crown (Kentucky Derby, Preakness and Belmont Stakes). The first – and to date the only – British-trained runner to be placed in the Kentucky Derby was Bold Arrangement, sent over by the ever-enterprising Clive Brittain (trainer of Pebbles) to finish second to Ferdinand in 1986. Dr Devious ran unplaced in the 1992 Kentucky Derby before landing 'the real thing' at Epsom, and that same Kentucky Derby saw the notorious flop of the French-trained Arazi, such a sensational winner of the Breeders' Cup Juvenile at the track the previous autumn.

A European horse finally graced the roll of honour of the US Triple Crown in 1990 when Go And Go, trained in Ireland by Dermot Weld and ridden by Mick Kinane, won the Belmont Stakes, and the same combination of trainer and jockey was responsible for another momentous breakthrough when in 1993 Vintage Crop became the first horse trained outside Australasia ever to win the Melbourne Cup, Australia's most famous race: Vintage Crop started 14–1 at Flemington and won by three lengths, an achievement which earned the horse a statue at The Curragh.

Serious bids by European horses for the Melbourne Cup are now a feature of racing in the autumn, and another Australian break-through for the raiders came in October 1998 when Taufan's Melody, trained by Lady Herries, ridden by Ray Cochrane and starting at 66–1, won the almost equally prestigious Caulfield Cup.

Hong Kong stages several extremely valuable invitational events, while the emergence of Japan as a major power in world racing has been reflected in the international fields gathered for the Japan Cup, run at the Fuchu track in Tokyo late in the year. The Japan Cup was first run in 1981, and in 1986 Jupiter Island became the first English-based winner – yet another reward for trainer Clive Brittain's policy of having a go. More recently the Japan Cup has gone to those great flyers of Michael Stoute's flag, Singspiel (1996) and Pilsudski (1997).

If the rise of Japan as a major force in world racing has been rapid, that of Dubai has been positively meteoric. Home of the Maktoum brothers (see page 60) and the base for their Godolphin operation, Dubai was a minor player in terms of actual races staged in the country until the establishment of the immensely valuable Dubai World Cup in 1996. The inaugural running was worth the equivalent of £1,586,627 to the winner, and the first three home gave the lie to the customary reluctance of top American trainers to race their horses abroad: the great Cigar (see page 113) won from fellow US challengers Soul Of The Matter and L'Carriere, with British-trained Pentire fourth. The 1997 running, postponed from its original date after torrential rain had washed out the course, went to British-trained Singspiel, and in 1998 it took another great American horse in the grey shape of Silver Charm (winner of the Kentucky Derby and Preakness in 1997) to withhold the late surge of Swain.

These big events hit the headlines, but a British trainer mounting a challenge for a handsome prize in North America or the Far East is now such an everyday occurrence that many well-known British horses are clocking up the air-miles and filling the coffers of their owners without drawing too much attention to their achievements. Yet mention must be made of one small trainer whose enterprise in 1998 paid off handsomely. Philip Mitchell thought so well of his colt Running Stag after he won the Winter Derby on the all-weather surface at Lingfield Park in March that he raced the horse in Germany and France as well as England before embarking on a bold attack on one of the biggest US races, the Woodward Stakes at Belmont Park: Running Stag covered himself in glory by finishing third behind Skip Away and Gentlemen (an effort which netted connections the equivalent of £28,351). He then finished fourth in the Jockey Club Gold Cup at the same track before running seventh in the Breeders' Cup Classic at Churchill Downs.

One-way traffic?

Notice something about the above chronicle of the gallant Brits on foreign soil? It's all about us going to take on them. When do they ever come over here to take on us? We're supposed to know all about Cigar and Silver Charm and Skip Away, but when do these horses come over here to play away from home and savour a taste of the Knavesmire or the Rowley Mile?

Although the traffic is not completely one-way, and although there are regular discussions about staging a European equivalent of the Breeders' Cup, few top American horses ever race in Europe. Reigh Count, winner of the Kentucky Derby in 1928, won the Coronation Cup in 1929, and Omaha, winner of the US Triple Crown in 1935, was narrowly defeated by Quashed in a famous race for the 1936 Ascot Gold Cup; but these were horses sent over well in advance to prepare for European campaigns. And 1936 is a long time ago.

Why the reluctance? There's the travel, of course, and the fact that in some states over there they are able to race on drugs prohibited over here. Then there's the prize money – why travel all the way to Europe to compete for a purse dwarfed by that for an equivalent race at home? – and the tracks: all the big races in North America are run on left-handed ovals, and most on dirt surfaces. To expect a horse who has made his reputation in such circumstances to put it on the line up the staring straight of Newmarket with heavy turf under-foot is asking a good deal, and despite the ultra-competitive nature of racing in the United States, few have felt moved to take up such a challenge. Fourstars Allstar, who took the Irish Two Thousand Guineas in 1991, is the only American-trained horse to have won a European Classic. The last American-trained runner in the Derby was Wolf Prince in 1993: Michael Dickinson's charge started at 40–1 and finished eighth behind Commander In Chief.

The sheer value and prestige of the Dubai World Cup, as we've seen, has attracted the cream of US racehorses, but the British racegoer is left to fantasise forlornly about a glimpse of the next Cigar in the flesh.

Seeking The Pearl became the first Japanese-trained horse ever to win a European Group One race when taking the Prix Maurice de Gheest at Deauville in August 1998. A week later Taki Shuttle became the second when winning the Prix Jacques Le Marois on the same course.

Jumping the water

Jump racing is far less international in terms of trainers in one country sending horses to compete in another. There is, of course, a great deal of to-ing and fro-ing across the Irish Sea; and François Doumen has spearheaded what has turned out to be practically a one-man French raiding party on the top staying chases. It all began with Nupsala, whose shock victory in the 1987 King George VI

Chase gave France its first jumping success in Britain for almost a quarter of a century, and the Doumen campaign continued with the great exploits of The Fellow, winner of the King George in 1991 and 1992 and eventually triumphant in the 1994 Cheltenham Gold Cup after being short-headed in the race in 1991 and 1992 and coming fourth in 1993. A fourth King George VI Chase in eight years fell to Doumen when Algan won the 1994 renewal after Barton Bank had deposited Adrian Maguire at the last.

Lonesome Glory became the first US-trained horse to win over the jumps in Great Britain when landing a hurdle race at Cheltenham in December 1992. Going in the other direction, Morley Street won the Breeders' Cup Steeplechase – an event with little of the razzmatazz of *the* Breeders' Cup – twice, and the Colonial Cup in Camden, South Carolina, often attracts overseas runners: that fine chaser Grand Canyon won it in 1976 and 1978.

The Grand National has such a worldwide reputation that it occasionally attracts raiders from afar: there have been a few Russian challengers for the race (though none with a serious chance), while the long tradition of American horsemen taking a tilt at Aintree's fences have produced victories since the Second World War for Tommy Smith on Jay Trump in 1965 and Charlie Fenwick on Ben Nevis in 1980. In both cases the horses were sent over well in advance to prepare for the race with top English trainers – Fred Winter for Jay Trump, Captain Tim Forster for Ben Nevis.

In the same spirit the Velka Pardubicka in the Czech Republic – that bizarre four-and-a-quarter-mile steeplechase which involves various strange fences and a stretch across a ploughed field – is now a regular target for adventurous British trainers: Charlie Mann rode It's A Snip to win the 1995 running.

The influence of international breeding

Competition between the major racing countries on the track may be hotting up, but the bloodstock world has had an international dimension for decades. Although the trend in the 1970s whereby many of the top European racehorses were exported to the United

States for their stud careers has abated with the revival of the breeding business in Europe, there is still a constant flow of blood-stock across the oceans. Some of the major movements include:

- *Exporting top European racehorses to Japan.* The exile of 1975 Derby winner Grundy to stand as a stallion in Japan after failing to make his mark in Britain was considered something of a come-down, and Dancing Brave (see page 115) ended up in Japan after his European stud career was blighted by illness. By the 1990s, however, while the export of a stallion to Japan may have been a cause for disappointment (since that horse would not be readily available to European breeders) it was no longer seen as a disgrace, and three consecutive Derby winners – Dr Devious, Commander In Chief and Erhaab – went straight to the land of the rising sun as soon as their three-year-old careers were over, though Dr Devious returned to stand at Coolmore in 1998. Generous, 1991 Derby winner, stood in England for a while before being exported to Japan in 1996, and another notable acquisition for Japanese breeders was Pilsudski (see opposite).

- *French-bred jumpers.* While Ireland is the traditional maternity ward for top steeplechasers, recent years have seen the growth of France as a breeding ground for National Hunt performers. The exploits of horses trained by François Doumen have advertised the potential of French-breds, but France has had a considerable influence on the jumping world for some time, with famous trainers such as Ryan Price and Peter Cazalet indulging in shrewd buying. Today Martin Pipe is at the vanguard of this cross-Channel trade, with well-known jumpers such as Rolling Ball, Challenger du Luc, Blowing Wind, Tamarindo, Eudipe and Cyfor Malta flying the tricolour on British racecourses.

- *The Australasian factor.* Like France, Australia and New Zealand play a significant role in the breeding of jumpers.

Five great globe-trotters

- **Triptych**, 'The Iron Lady', trained for most of her career in France by Patrick-Louis Biancone, ran in forty-one races – thirty-five of them Group One or Grade One – in six countries between 1984 and 1988: France, Britain, Ireland, the United States, Canada and Japan. Her fourteen victories included the Coronation Cup twice, Champion Stakes twice, International Stakes, Irish Two Thousand Guineas and Phoenix Champion Stakes.
- **Snurge**, trained at Whatcombe by Paul Cole, won prize money in six countries between 1989 and 1994: Britain (including the 1990 St Leger), Ireland, France, Italy, Germany and Canada.
- **Singspiel**, trained at Newmarket by Michael Stoute, won Group One races in four countries between 1994 and 1997: Britain (including the Coronation Cup and International Stakes), Canada (Canadian International), Dubai (Dubai World Cup) and Japan (Japan Cup).
- **Pilsudski**, also trained by Michael Stoute, won major races in Britain (including the Eclipse Stakes and Champion Stakes in 1997), Ireland (1997 Irish Champion Stakes), Canada (1996 Breeders' Cup Turf), Germany and Japan (1997 Japan Cup). He was twice second in the Prix de l'Arc de Triomphe.
- **Luso**, trained at Newmarket by Clive Brittain, may not have been quite in the same bracket as the above four in terms of sheer ability, but his itinerary over five years of racing between 1994 and his retirement in 1998 epitomised the globe-trotting racehorse. He won ten races in four countries: Britain, Italy (where he landed the 1995 Derby Italiano), Germany and Hong Kong (where he twice won the International Vase). Luso, who earned almost £2 million for his connections, also raced in France, and took part twice in the Dubai World Cup. Only eleven of his thirty-four career starts were in Britain.

The best Australian chaser to race in Britain in recent memory was the great Crisp, narrowly beaten by Red Rum in the 1973 Grand National, and several top-notch performers have been New Zealand-bred, including two recent Grand National winners: Seagram (1991) and Lord Gyllene (1997). Other familiar jumpers bred in New Zealand are Grand Canyon, Playschool and 1980 Whitbread Gold Cup winner Royal Mail.

The southern hemisphere has benefited from improvements in air travel by receiving European-based stallions to stand in Australia or New Zealand outside the European covering season. Ahonoora, sire of 1992 Derby winner Dr Devious, was a pioneer of such dual-centre activity, and 1991 Arc winner Suave Dancer was on his third stint away from the National Stud in Newmarket when he was killed by a lightning strike at stud near Melbourne in December 1998.

Index